pumpkin

horse

Children's Dictionary

3,000 Words, Pictures, and Definitions

Editor: Martin Manser
Associate Editor: Alice Grandison

FOR YOUNG READERS

slippers

handbag

kick

Welcome to this dictionary!

This dictionary is suitable for children age six or seven and up. It's a fun way for children to learn about words. Children will find the dictionary easy to use, with its clearly explained meanings and its attractive layout. An extra feature is the many colorful illustrations and photographs, which really bring the meanings of the words to life. Each page has the letters of the alphabet listed down the sides, to help you quickly find the word you are looking up.

The headwords are the words that you look up. These are shown in **bold** type:

joke noun (plural **jokes**) something funny that a person says or does to make people laugh.

For each headword, a part of speech (word class) is shown—noun, verb, adjective, adverb or preposition:

wish verb (**wishes; wishing; wished**) want something to happen: I wish I had a puppy.

After each headword is the meaning (definition) of the word:

timid adjective shy and easily frightened.

If a headword has more than one meaning, the different meanings are numbered:

mouse noun (plural **mice**) **1** a small, furry animal with a long tail. **2** a small object that you use to move things around on a computer screen.

If a headword has more than one part of speech, the second part of speech is shown below the first, with a bullet point before it:

taste noun (plural **tastes**) **1** the flavor of something: a salty taste. **2** the ability to recognize flavors.
• verb (**tastes; tasting; tasted**) **1** (of food or a drink) have a particular kind of flavor: This curry tastes very spicy. **2** eat or drink a little bit of something to see whether you like it.

Children's Dictionary

Racehorse for Young Readers™ books may be purchased in bulk at special discounts for sales promotion, corporate gifts, fund-raising, or educational purposes. Special editions can also be created to specifications. For details, contact the Special Sales Department, Skyhorse Publishing, 307 West 36th Street, 11th Floor, New York, NY 10018 or info@skyhorsepublishing.com.

Racehorse for Young Readers™ is a pending trademark of Skyhorse Publishing, Inc.®, a Delaware corporation.

Visit our website at www.skyhorsepublishing.com.

10 9 8 7 6 5 4 3

Library of Congress Cataloging-in-Publication Data is available on file.

Photo credits: Shutterstock
Cover design: Mona Lin

ISBN: 978-1-6315-8273-8

Printed in China

Many headwords have helpful examples showing how the word can be used in a sentence or phrase. These examples are shown in smaller type:

afford verb **(affords; affording; afforded)** have enough money to buy something: We can't afford a new car.

Other forms of the headword are shown after the part of speech.

When the headword is a noun (a naming word), the plural form is shown:

tomato noun (plural **tomatoes**) a small, soft, round, red fruit that can be eaten raw or cooked.

When the headword is a verb (a doing word), the form of the present tense used with *he*, *she* or *it* (the third person singular), the present participle (the *–ing* form), and the past tense and past participle are shown:

shiver verb **(shivers; shivering; shivered)** tremble because you are cold or afraid.

If a verb has a past participle (for example *written* in *I have written*) that is different from the past tense, this is also shown:

write verb **(writes; writing; wrote; written)** put words onto a piece of paper using a pen or pencil.

When the headword is an adjective (a describing word), the comparative (the *-er* form) and superlative (the *-est* form) are shown:

tiny adjective **(tinier; tiniest)** very small.

abandon verb (**abandons; abandoning; abandoned**) leave someone forever: The man abandoned his wife and child.

abbreviation noun (plural **abbreviations**) a short way of writing a word or phrase: "Rd." is an abbreviation of "road."

ability noun (plural **abilities**) being able to do something: the ability to fly.

abroad adverb to another country: We are going abroad this summer.

absent adjective not present; away: absent from school.

absolutely adverb very; completely: Are you absolutely sure?

absorb verb (**absorbs; absorbing; absorbed**) soak up a liquid.

accent noun (plural **accents**) the way people from a particular place speak: an Irish accent.

accept verb (**accepts; accepting; accepted**) take something that someone offers you: Tom offered Julia a candy and she accepted.

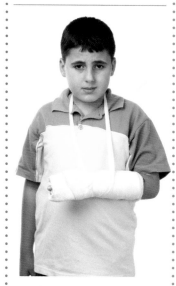

accident noun (plural **accidents**) something bad or painful that happens without anyone meaning it to happen: He stood on my foot by accident.

accurate adjective correct in every detail: an accurate report.

accuse verb (**accuses; accusing; accused**) say that you think someone has done something wrong: He accused me of stealing his pencil.

ache verb (**aches; aching; ached**) be painful: My back is aching.

acid noun (plural **acids**) a very strong liquid that can burn you.

act verb (**acts; acting; acted**) **1** behave in a particular way: He was acting like a fool. **2** play a part in a film or a play.

action noun (plural **actions**) something that you do: His brave action saved the child's life.

active adjective energetic and busy.

activity noun (plural **activities**) something that people do for fun: activities such as painting, soccer, and swimming.

actor noun (plural **actors**) a person who plays a part in a film or a play.

actress noun (plural **actresses**) a woman or girl who plays a part in a film or a play.

actually adverb really: Are you actually going to Disney World?

add verb (**adds; adding; added**) **1** put something with something else: She added milk to her tea. **2** count numbers together to find out the total: 2 added to 3 makes 5.

address noun (plural **addresses**) **1** your house number, street, and town. **2** the set of letters and numbers that you use when you send someone an email.

admire verb (**admires; admiring; admired**) **1** think well of someone: We all admire John because he is so smart. **2** look at something with pleasure: They were admiring the view.

admit verb (**admits; admitting; admitted**) say that you have done something wrong: Matthew admitted that he had told a lie.

adopt verb (**adopts; adopting; adopted**) take someone else's child into your family and raise them as your own child: The Millers adopted Donna when she was a baby.

adult noun (plural **adults**) a man or woman; a grown-up

advantage noun (plural **advantages**) something about you that makes you more likely to do better than other people: Being tall is an advantage for a basketball player.

adventure noun (plural **adventures**) something exciting that you do.

advertisement noun (plural **advertisements**) a short film or a picture that tries to persuade people to buy something.

advise verb (**advises; advising; advised**) tell someone what you think they should do: I advise you to tell the truth.

affect verb (**affects; affecting; affected**) make someone or something different in some way: The village was badly affected by the floods.

afford verb (**affords; affording; afforded**) have enough money to buy something: We can't afford a new car.

afraid adjective worried that something bad might happen; frightened.

afternoon noun (plural **afternoons**) the part of the day between morning and evening.

age noun (plural **ages**) how old you are.

agree verb (**agrees; agreeing; agreed**) think the same as someone else about something.

aid noun help: A kind man came to our aid when our car broke down.

aim verb (**aims; aiming; aimed**) point a weapon or other object at someone or something.

air noun the gases all around us, which we breathe.

air force noun (plural **air forces**) an organized group of people who fight for their country in airplanes if there is a war.

airplane noun (plural **airplanes**) a vehicle with wings and an engine that flies through the air.

alien noun (plural **aliens**) in a story, a creature from another planet.

airport noun (plural **airports**) a place where you start and end a journey by airplane.

album noun (plural albums) a book where you keep photographs or stamps.

alike adjective very similar in some way: The two sisters look alike.

alive adjective living; not dead.

allergy noun (plural **allergies**) a bad reaction from your body (such as sneezing, itching, or difficulty breathing) to a particular food or animal: I have an allergy to strawberries.

alligator noun (plural **alligators**) an animal that looks like a smaller crocodile and that lives in water.

allow verb (**allows; allowing; allowed**) let someone do something: I am not allowed to cross the street on my own.

alone adjective by yourself; without anyone else.

aloud adverb loud enough to be heard: The teacher asked Lisa to read aloud to the class.

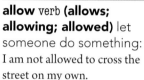

alphabet noun (plural **alphabets**) all the letters that are used to write words, ordered from A to Z.

alter verb (**alters; altering; altered**) change something.

aluminum noun a lightweight, silver-colored metal.

amazing adjective very surprising, in a good way.

ambition noun (plural **ambitions**) something that you really hope to do in the future: My ambition is to be a famous author.

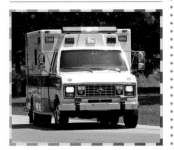

ambulance noun (plural **ambulances**) a vehicle that takes sick people to the hospital.

amount noun (plural **amounts**) how much there is of something: a huge amount of money.

amuse verb (**amuses; amusing; amused**) make someone laugh.

anchor noun (plural **anchors**) a large, heavy, metal hook on a chain, which is dropped over the side of a boat to stop it from moving.

ancient adjective very old.

angel noun (plural **angels**) a being that some people believe lives in heaven with God.

anger noun a strong feeling of annoyance.

angle noun (plural **angles**) a corner where two lines meet.

angry adjective (**angrier; angriest**) very annoyed.

animal see page 10.

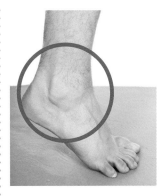

ankle noun (plural **ankles**) the joint between your foot and your leg.

anniversary noun (plural **anniversaries**) a date when you remember something important that happened on the same date in an earlier year: a wedding anniversary.

announce verb (**announces; announcing; announced**) tell people about something important: The principal announced that the school would close early because of the heavy snow.

annoy verb (**annoys; annoying; annoyed**) make someone irritated or angry.

annual adjective happening once a year: our annual holiday.
+ noun (plural **annuals**) a book that comes out once a year.

answer verb (**answers; answering; answered**) say something to someone who has asked

a question: Dad asked if I would like a drink and I answered, "Yes, please."
+ noun (plural **answers**) what you say to someone who has asked a question.

ant noun (plural **ants**) a tiny insect that lives in a large group.

antelope noun (plural **antelopes**) an animal that looks like a deer with large horns.

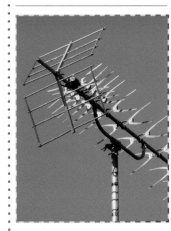

antenna noun (plural **antennas**) a wire that receives radio or television signals.

anxious adjective worried and nervous.

A B C D E F G H I J K L M N O P Q R S T U V W X Y Z

animal

noun (plural **animals**) any living thing other than a plant.

lion

cat

dog

frog

cow

snake

giraffe

rhinoceros

monkey

rabbit

donkey

toad

tiger

impala

orangutan

sheep

warthog

lizard

mountain goat

pig

kangaroo

leopard

baboon

wildebeest

dolphin

zebra

brown bear

hyena

wolf

arctic fox

bison

gorilla

coyote

killer whale

crocodile

camel

polar bear

otter

koi carp

river turtle

salamander

walrus

seal

ape noun (plural **apes**) an animal that looks like a large monkey without a tail.

apologize verb (**apologizes; apologizing; apologized**) say you are sorry for something that you have done: Sarah apologized for being late.

appear verb (**appears; appearing; appeared**) **1** come into view: The bus appeared at the end of the street. **2** seem to be something: She appeared to be angry.

appearance noun (plural **appearances**) the way someone or something looks: She takes great care with her appearance.

appetite noun (plural **appetites**) a feeling that you want to eat: He lost his appetite when he was ill.

applause noun clapping your hands to show that you enjoyed something.

apple noun (plural **apples**) a round, crunchy fruit that grows on a tree.

appointment noun (plural **appointments**) an arrangement to meet with someone.

appreciate verb (**appreciates; appreciating; appreciated**) be grateful for something: I appreciate your kindness.

approach verb (**approaches; approaching; approached**) come near to a place or a person.

approve verb (**approves; approving; approved**) think that something is good: She does not approve of people wearing fur.

approximately adverb about; not exactly: approximately twenty minutes.

apricot noun (plural **apricots**) a small, round, soft, yellowish-orange fruit.

apron noun (plural **aprons**) a piece of material that you wear over your clothes to keep them clean when you are cooking.

aquarium noun (plural **aquariums**) a glass tank for keeping fish in.

arch noun (plural **arches**) a curved part of a building or bridge.

area noun (plural **areas**) a part of a city or country: a rough area of London.

argue verb (**argues; arguing; argued**) talk angrily with someone because you do not agree with them.

argument noun (plural **arguments**) an angry talk in which people do not agree with each other.

arithmetic noun sums with numbers.

arm noun (plural **arms**) one of two long parts of your body that start at your shoulders and end at your hands.

armor noun heavy metal suits that soldiers wore in battle a long time ago.

arrive verb (**arrives; arriving; arrived**) come to a place: Holly arrived at the party early.

arrow noun (plural **arrows**) a thin stick with a point on the end that is fired from a bow.

article noun (plural **articles**) **1** an object; thing. **2** a story in a newspaper or magazine.

artificial adjective not real; made by human beings: an artificial leg.

something out by putting a question to someone: "What time is it?" she asked. **2** tell someone that you want them to give you something: I asked my mom for an apple.

army noun (plural **armies**) an organized group of people who fight for their country on land if there is a war.

artist noun (plural **artists**) a person who paints pictures or makes sculptures.

asleep adjective having your eyes closed and your body completely at rest; sleeping.

arrange verb (**arranges; arranging; arranged**) **1** make plans for something to happen: The bride and groom are arranging their wedding. **2** put things in a neat or pretty order: The flowers were beautifully arranged.

art noun drawing, painting, and sculpture.

ash noun (plural **ashes**) **1** the gray dust that is left after a fire. **2** a large tree with broad leaves.

ashamed adjective feeling guilty about something bad that you have done.

arrest verb (**arrests; arresting; arrested**) (of a police officer) take someone to the police station because they have broken a law.

ask verb (**asks; asking; asked**) **1** try to find

assembly noun (plural **assemblies**) a meeting of the whole school.

assistant noun (plural **assistants**) **1** a person who helps someone in their work: The classroom assistant helps the teacher. **2** a person who serves customers in a shop.

asthma noun an illness that makes it hard sometimes for you to breathe properly.

astonish verb (**astonishes**; **astonishing**; **astonished**) surprise someone very much.

astronaut noun (plural **astronauts**) a person who is trained to travel in space.

athletics noun contests in running, jumping, and throwing.

atlas noun (plural **atlases**) a book of maps.

atmosphere noun (plural **atmospheres**) **1** the layer of air around the earth. **2** the mood in a place: There was an exciting atmosphere in the theatre.

attach verb (**attaches**; **attaching**; **attached**) join something onto another thing: I attached an address label to my suitcase.

attack verb (**attacks**; **attacking**; **attacked**) try to hurt or injure someone.

attempt verb (**attempts**; **attempting**; **attempted**) try to do something: The girl attempted to lift the heavy bag.

attend verb (**attends**; **attending**; **attended**) go to school, church, etc.: We attend the local school.

attention noun listening or watching carefully: You must pay attention to what your teacher says.

attic noun (plural **attics**) a room at the top of a house, just below the roof.

attractive adjective nice to look at; pretty or handsome.

audience noun (plural **audiences**) the people who are watching a show, a play, or a film.

aunt noun (plural **aunts**) your mother's or father's sister, or your uncle's wife.

author noun (plural **authors**) a person who writes a book.

autograph noun (plural **autographs**) signing your name, especially when a famous person signs their name on a piece of paper for someone to keep.

automatic adjective working on its own; not controlled by a person: automatic doors.

autumn noun (plural **autumns**) the part of the year between summer and winter, when the leaves fall off the trees.

available adjective possible to get or use: There are still some tickets available for the concert.

avalanche noun (plural **avalanches**) a large amount snow and stones sliding down a mountainside.

avenue noun (plural **avenues**) a wide street with trees on each side.

average adjective ordinary; not unusual: a girl of average height.

avoid verb (**avoids; avoiding; avoided**) stay away from someone or something.

awake adjective not asleep.

award noun (plural **awards**) a prize given to someone for winning a contest or for doing something well: an award for writing the best story.

aware adjective knowing something: I was aware that someone was hiding in the shadows.

awful adjective very bad; terrible: an awful pain.

awkward adjective **1** difficult to do or use: This big box is very awkward to carry. **2** (of a person) moving in a clumsy way.

axe noun (plural **axes**) a tool with a long, wooden handle and a sharp, heavy, metal blade for chopping wood.

baby noun (plural **babies**) a very young child.

back noun (plural **backs**) **1** the part of your body that is behind you, from your neck to your bottom. **2** the part of an animal's body that is on top, from its head to its tail. **3** the part of something that is opposite the front: the back of the bus.
+ adverb again: We went back to France.

background noun (plural **backgrounds**) the part of a picture that is behind the main part.

backpack noun (plural **backpacks**) a bag with shoulder straps, which you wear on your back.

bacon noun salted meat that comes from a pig.

bad adjective (**worse; worst**) **1** (of a person) nasty or wicked. **2** unpleasant or horrible: I've had a bad day. **3** (of food) no longer fresh and safe to eat.

badge noun (plural **badges**) a small object that you wear attached to your clothes, sometimes to show that you are a member of a certain group.

bag noun (plural **bags**) a container that you keep your things in and that you carry around with you.

bake verb (**bakes; baking; baked**) cook bread, cakes, etc. in the oven.

balance verb (**balances; balancing; balanced**) stay steady, without falling over: The man was balancing on a narrow ledge.

bald adjective **(balder; baldest)** having no hair on your head.

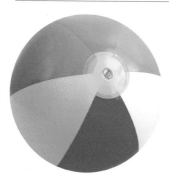

ball noun (plural **balls**) **1** a round object that you throw, kick, or hit in games. **2** large, fancy party with dancing.

ballet noun a kind of dancing in which you dance on the tips of your toes.

balloon noun (plural **balloons)** a light rubber bag that you blow air into so that it grows bigger, which can be used as a toy or a decoration.

ban verb **(bans; banning; banned)** not allow something to be done: *Smoking is banned in public places.*

banana noun **(plural bananas)** a long , curved fruit with a yellow skin and a soft, whitish inside part which you can eat.

band noun (plural **bands**) **1** a group of people who play music together. **2** a thin strip of rubber, cotton or other material.

bandage noun (plural **bandages)** a strip of material that you wrap around a part of your body that you have hurt, to keep it clean.

bang noun (plural **bangs)** a sudden, loud noise. + verb **(bangs; banging; banged)** make a sudden, loud noise: *The back door banged.*

bank noun (plural **banks**) **1** a place where people can keep their money safely: *I am saving all my money in the bank.* **2** the sloping ground on either side of a river.

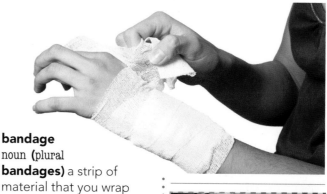

bar noun (plural **bars**) **1** a long piece of metal or wood: *an iron bar.* **2** a block of chocolate, soap, etc. **3** a place where you can buy drinks or food: *a coffee bar.*

barbecue noun (plural **barbecues) 1** a metal frame on which you cook food outside over a fire. **2** an outdoor party where people cook food on a barbecue.

bare adjective **(barer; barest) 1** not covered by clothes: *bare feet.* **2** (of a place) having nothing in it or on it: *a bare room.*

bark verb **(barks; barking; barked)** (of a dog) make a rough, loud noise.

+ noun the rough covering of the trunk of a tree.

barrel noun (plural **barrels**) a large, round, wooden or metal container for holding liquids.

barrier noun (plural **barriers**) a fence, wall, etc. that stops people from getting past it.

basin noun (plural **basins**) a container shaped like a large bowl.

basket noun (plural **baskets**) a container made from strips of wood or straw, which you carry things in.

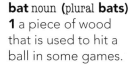

bat noun (plural **bats**)
1 a piece of wood that is used to hit a ball in some games.

2 a small animal that looks like a mouse with wings, which flies at night.

bath noun (plural **baths**) a container with water taps that you can lie in to wash your whole body.

battery noun (plural **batteries**) an object that stores electricity and makes a watch, radio, mobile phone, etc. work.

battle noun (plural **battles**) a fight between armies at war.

beach noun (plural **beaches**) the land at the edge of the sea, which is covered in sand or small stones.

bead noun (plural **beads**) a small piece of plastic or glass with a hole through it: a necklace of orange beads.

beak noun (plural **beaks**) the hard outer part of a bird's mouth.

bean noun (plural **beans**)
1 a pod with seeds inside, which is eaten as a vegetable. **2** a seed that grows inside a pod, which is eaten as a vegetable.

bear noun (plural **bears**) a big, strong, wild animal with thick fur and sharp claws.

beard noun (plural **beards**) the hair that grows on the lower part of a man's face.

beat verb (**beats; beating; beat; beaten**) **1** win a game or contest against someone: Andrew beat his brother at tennis. **2** hit someone hard several times. **3** (of your heart) make a regular sound.

beautiful adjective very pleasing to look at.

bed noun (plural **beds**) **1** a piece of furniture that you sleep on. **2** the bottom of the sea or of a river.

beef noun meat that comes from a cow.

beetle noun (plural **beetles**) an insect with hard wings.

bee noun (plural **bees**) a flying insect that makes a buzzing sound and makes honey from the pollen it collects from flowers.

beg verb (**begs; begging; begged**) ask someone eagerly to do something: I begged them to help me.

begin verb (**begins; beginning; began; begun**) start: The film begins at six o'clock.

behave verb (**behaves; behaving; behaved**) act in a particular way: Tom was behaving like a fool.

believe verb (**believes; believing; believed**) think

that something is true: The teacher didn't believe his excuse for being late.

bell noun (plural **bells**) a metal object that makes a ringing sound when something knocks against it.

belt noun (plural **belts**) a band, usually of leather, that you wear around your waist.

bench noun (plural **benches**) a long seat in a public place that a few people can sit on.

bend verb (**bends; bending; bent**) **1** make something into a curved shape: Bend your knees.

2 lean forward and downwards: I bent down to tie my shoelaces.
✦ noun (plural **bends**) a curved part of a road.

berry noun (plural **berries**) a small, round, soft fruit with seeds in it.

best adjective better than all the others: the best soccer player in the world.

better adjective more skillful than another: Your drawing is better than mine.

beware verb be careful of something that is dangerous: Beware of the dog.

bicycle noun (plural **bicycles**) a vehicle with two wheels and no engine, which you pedal with your feet.

big adjective (**bigger; biggest**) of great size; not small.

bill noun (plural **bills**) **1** a piece of paper that shows how much money you have to pay for something: the phone bill. **2** the hard outer part of a bird's mouth; a beak.

bin noun (plural **bins**) a container used for storage.

bird see page 22.

birthday noun (plural **birthdays**) the day of your birth or the anniversary of the day of your birth each year.

biscuit noun (plural **biscuits**) a kind of small, light bread.

bit noun (plural **bits**) a small piece of something: a bit of paper.

bite verb (**bites; biting; bit; bitten**) cut something with your teeth: I bit off a piece of apple.

bitter adjective having an unpleasant, sour taste.

black adjective (**blacker; blackest**) of the darkest color, like the sky at night.

blackboard noun (plural **blackboards**) a dark-colored board that you can write on with chalk.

blade noun (plural **blades**) **1** the sharp metal part of a knife or sword. **2** a single piece of grass.

blame verb (**blames; blaming; blamed**) say that it is someone's fault that something bad happened: Mom blamed me for making the baby cry.

blank adjective (**blanker; blankest**) (of a piece of paper) having no writing or other marks on it.

blanket noun (plural **blankets**) a warm bed cover.

blazer noun (plural **blazers**) a kind of jacket that looks like a suit jacket but is not worn as part of a suit: my school uniform blazer.

bleed verb (**bleeds; bleeding; bled**) (of part of your body) have blood coming out of it: I cut my finger and it started bleeding.

blind adjective not able to see.

blink verb (**blinks; blinking; blinked**) close and open your eyes very quickly.

blister noun (plural **blisters**) a small, painful lump on your skin with liquid inside it: My new shoes have rubbed against my toes and given me blisters.

blizzard noun (plural **blizzards**) a storm with very heavy snow and a strong wind.

block noun (plural **blocks**) **1** a large piece of stone, wood, etc.: a block of ice. **2** an area of land surrounded by four streets in a city.
+ verb (**blocks; blocking; blocked**) put something in a road, pipe, etc., so that

nothing can get past: There was a large truck across the road, blocking it.

blond adjective (of a man or boy) having light-colored hair.

blonde adjective (of a woman or girl) having light-colored hair.

bird
noun (plural **birds**) a creature with two legs, wings, feathers and a beak.

toucan

starling

partridge

pigeon

robin

swan

turkey

emu

hoopoe

owl

kiwi

parrot

puffin

flamingo

a b c d e f g h i j k l m n o p q r s t u v w x y z

22

duck

penguin

magpie

hawk

rooster

parakeet

ostrich

eagle

pelican

quetzal

macaw

vulture

goose

blood noun the red liquid that your heart pumps inside your body.

blouse noun (plural **blouses**) a piece of clothing like a shirt, worn by women and girls.

blow verb (**blows; blowing; blew; blown**) **1** force air out of your mouth. **2** (of the wind) make the air move. + noun (plural **blows**) a hard hit or punch.

blue adjective (**bluer; bluest**) of the color of the sky on a sunny day.
blunt adjective (**blunter;**

bluntest) not sharp: My pencil is blunt.

blur noun (plural **blurs**) something that you cannot see clearly: Without my glasses, everything was a blur.

blush verb (**blushes; blushing; blushed**) go red in the face because you feel shy or embarrassed.

board noun (plural **boards**) a flat, rectangular, rigid piece of wood or other material.

boast verb (**boasts; boasting; boasted**) talk too proudly about the things you own or the things you are good at: He is always boasting about his big house.

boat noun (plural **boats**) a small vessel that travels on water.

body noun (plural **bodies**) **1** your whole self, from head to foot: My whole body ached. **2** the part of your body that does not include your head, arms and legs. **3** a dead person.

boil verb (**boils; boiling; boiled**) **1** (of a liquid) bubble and turn into steam because it is very hot. **2** cook food in boiling water: Boil the potatoes.

bomb noun (plural **bombs**) a weapon that explodes and can cause a lot of damage to people and buildings.

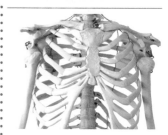

bone noun (plural **bones**) one of the hard, white parts inside your body that make up your skeleton.

bonfire noun (plural **bonfires**) a large fire that you make outdoors.

book noun (plural **books**) a number of printed pages that are bound together inside a cover. **+** verb (**books; booking; booked**) arrange for something to be kept for you: We booked tickets for the theatre.

boot noun (plural **boots**) a shoe that comes up over your ankle and sometimes up to your knee.

border noun (**plural borders**) **1** the place where the edges of two states or countries meet; a boundary: the border between the US and Canada. **2** the edge of an object, sometimes having a decoration: a white plate with a gold border.

boring adjective dull and uninteresting.

born adjective having come out of your mother's body and started your life: Ryan was born in Ireland.

borrow verb (**borrows; borrowing; borrowed**) get something that belongs to someone else and give it back to them after a while: I borrowed a pencil from Sophie for the afternoon.

boss noun (plural **bosses**) the person who is in charge at a place of work.

bother verb (**bothers; bothering; bothered**) **1** make someone feel worried or annoyed: I hope the dog's barking is not bothering you. **2** make an effort to do something: He didn't bother to wipe his feet.

bottle noun (plural **bottles**) a container for liquids, usually made of glass or plastic.

bottom noun (plural **bottoms**) **1** the lowest part of something: the bottom of the swimming pool. **2** the part of your body that you sit on.

boulder noun (plural **boulders**) a very large rock.

bounce verb (**bounces; bouncing; bounced**) spring back up after hitting something: The ball bounced off the ground.

boundary noun (plural **boundaries**) the edge of a piece of land.

bow noun (plural **bows**) **1** a knot with two large loops. **2** a curved piece of wood with a string attached to both ends, which is used to fire arrows. **+** verb (**bows; bowing; bowed**) bend your body forward at the waist to show respect to someone.

bowl noun (plural **bowls**) a deep rounded dish for holding food or liquid: a bowl of soup.

box noun (plural **boxes**) a container made of wood, cardboard, or plastic, used for storing things: Put all your things away in the toy box.

bracelet noun (plural **bracelets**) a piece of jewelery that you wear around your wrist.

brain noun (plural **brains**) the part of your body, inside your head, that controls your thoughts and movements.

brake noun (plural **brakes**) the part of a vehicle that slows it down or stops it from moving.

branch noun (plural **branches**) a part of a tree that grows out from its trunk.

brave adjective (**braver; bravest**) willing to do things that are dangerous or frightening.

bread noun a kind of food that is made from flour and water and is baked in an oven.

break verb (**breaks; breaking; broke; broken**) smash or damage something.
+ noun (plural **breaks**) a short rest.

breakfast noun (plural **breakfasts**) the first meal of the day.

breathe verb (**breathes; breathing; breathed**) take air into your lungs and let air out of your lungs through your nose or mouth.

breeze noun (plural **breezes**) a light wind.

brick noun (plural **bricks**) a block made from baked clay that is used for building.

bride noun (plural **brides**) a woman who is getting married.

bridge noun (plural **bridges**) something that is built across a river or road so that people can walk or drive across it.

brief adjective (**briefer; briefest**) lasting a very short time: a brief visit.

bright adjective (**brighter; brightest**) **1** (of a light) shining with a lot of light. **2** (of a color) strong and clear; not dull. **3** (of a person) able to learn and understand things quickly; clever.

brilliant adjective **1** (of a light or color) very bright. **2** (of a person) very clever or talented: a brilliant pianist.

bring verb (**brings; bringing; brought**) take something or someone with you to a place.

broad adjective (**broader; broadest**) very wide: a broad river.

broccoli noun a dark green vegetable.

brooch noun (plural **brooches**) a piece of jewelry that you wear pinned to your clothes.

brother noun (plural **brothers**) a man or boy who has the same parents as you.

brown adjective (**browner; brownest**) of the color of earth.

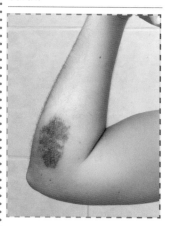

bruise noun (plural **bruises**) a dark mark on the skin where it has been hit or knocked.

brush noun (plural **brushes**) an object with bristles attached to a handle, used for sweeping floors, cleaning your teeth, smoothing your hair, etc.

bubble noun (plural **bubbles**) a small ball of air inside a liquid.

bucket noun (plural **buckets**) a large metal or plastic container with a handle, often used for carrying water.

buckle noun (plural **buckles**) a metal or plastic fastening on a belt or strap.

build verb (**builds; building; built**) make something by joining parts together: The men built a brick wall.

building noun (plural **buildings**) a place that has been built with walls and a roof.

bulb noun (plural **bulbs**) **1** the glass part of an electric lamp that gives out light. **2** the onion-shaped root of some plants that grow under the ground.

bulge verb (**bulges; bulging; bulged**) stick out in a curved shape: His pockets are bulging with candy.

bull noun (plural **bulls**) a male cow, elephant, or whale.

bullet noun (plural **bullets**) a small metal object that is fired from a gun.

bully noun (plural **bullies**) a person who frightens or is unkind to weaker people.

bump verb (**bumps; bumping; bumped**) hit or knock into something: I bumped into the table. + noun (plural **bumps**) **1** the sound of something falling to the ground; a knock. **2** a lump on the surface of something: a bump in the road.

bunch noun (plural **bunches**) a group of things joined together: a bunch of bananas.

bundle noun (plural **bundles**) a group of things joined together: a bundle of papers.

bunk beds noun two beds joined together, one above the other.

burglar noun (plural **burglars**) a person who breaks into people's houses and steals things.

burn verb (**burns; burning; burned** or **burnt**) **1** damage or destroy something by fire. **2** injure yourself by contact with fire or something hot: I burned my finger on the stove.

burrow noun (plural **burrows**) a hole in the ground where an animal lives.

burst verb (**bursts; bursting; burst**) suddenly break open: The balloon burst with a loud bang.

bury verb (**buries; burying; buried**) put a dead body or an object in a hole in the ground and cover it up.

butcher noun (plural **butchers**) a person who cuts up meat and sells it.

butter noun a yellowish fat made from cream, which can be spread on bread.

butterfly noun (plural **butterflies**) an insect with large colorful wings.

button noun (plural **buttons**) **1** a small object used to fasten clothing by pushing it through a small hole. **2** a part of a machine that you press to make it work.

buy verb (**buys; buying; bought**) get something by paying money for it.

buzz verb (**buzzes; buzzing; buzzed**) make a humming sound like a bee.

cab noun (plural **cabs**) **1** the front part of a truck, bus, or train, where the driver sits. **2** a taxi.

cabbage noun (plural **cabbages**) a large vegetable with green leaves that form a rounded shape.

cabin noun (plural **cabins**) **1** a room for passengers and crew on a ship or airplane. **2** a small wooden house or hut, often in the mountains.

cable noun (plural **cables**) **1** a strong, thick rope made of twisted wire. **2** a bundle of wires that carry electricity.

cactus noun (plural **cactuses** or **cacti**) a plant with spines but no leaves, which grows in hot, dry places.

café noun (plural **cafés**) a small restaurant that sells snacks and drinks.

cage noun (plural **cages**) a container with metal bars where birds or animals are kept.

cake noun (plural **cakes**) a sweet food that is made from flour, butter, eggs, and sugar, and is baked in the oven.

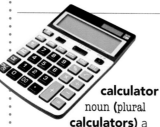

calculator noun (plural **calculators**) a small electronic machine used for doing sums.

calendar noun (plural **calendars**) a chart that shows the year divided into days, weeks, and months.

calf noun (plural **calves**) **1** a young cow, elephant, or whale. **2** the back part of your leg between the knee and the ankle.

call verb (**calls; calling; called**) **1** shout to attract someone's attention: I heard someone calling for help.
2 give someone a name: They called the baby Jack. **3** telephone someone: I'll call you tonight.

calm adjective (**calmer; calmest**) **1** not windy: a calm day. **2** not showing anger or excitement: Keep calm!

camel noun (plural **camels**) an animal with a long neck and one or two humps on its back, which is used to carry people in the desert.

camera noun (plural **cameras**) a device used for taking photographs or moving pictures.

camp noun (plural **camps**) a place where people stay for a short time in tents or cabins: a summer camp. verb (**camps; camping; camped**) stay for a short time in a tent or cabin: We went camping for the weekend.

can verb (**could**) be able to do something: She can speak French.
+ noun (plural **cans**) a metal container holding food or a drink: a can of peas.

canal noun (plural **canals**) a stretch of water that has been built for boats to travel along.

cancel verb (**cancels; canceling; canceled**) stop an arrangement from happening: I canceled my appointment.

candle noun (plural **candles**) an object made of wax with a piece of string inside that can be set alight to provide light.

canoe noun (plural **canoes**) a long, light, narrow boat that is moved by using a paddle.

cap noun (plural **caps**) **1** a soft hat with a stiff part sticking out at the front. **2** the lid of a bottle or other container.

capital noun (plural **capitals**) **1** the city where the government is located in a state or country: Rome is the capital of Italy. **2** the uppercase letter that is used at the beginning of a sentence or a name.

capture verb (**captures; capturing; captured**) take someone prisoner.

car noun (plural **cars**) a motor vehicle with four wheels for a small number of people to travel in.

caravan noun (plural **caravans**) group of people or animals traveling together on a long journey.

card noun (plural **cards**) **1** material like thick, stiff paper. **2** a piece of card with a picture on it, which you send to someone with a message: a birthday card. **3** one of a set of small pieces of card with numbers or pictures on them, which are used to play games.

cardboard noun material like thick, stiff paper, often used to make boxes.

cardigan noun (plural **cardigans**) a knitted jacket that fastens with buttons at the front.

care verb (**cares; caring; cared**) **1** think something is important; mind: I don't care if we go to the movies or go bowling. **2** look after someone: A nurse cares for sick people.

career noun (plural **careers**) the kind of work that someone does: a career in the police force.

careful adjective paying close attention so as to avoid danger or mistakes: Be careful crossing the road!

careless adjective not paying close attention to what you are doing: You've made a careless mistake in this math problem.

caretaker noun (plural **caretakers**) a person who looks after property for someone else.

carnival noun (plural **carnivals**) festival that may include rides and games or a show.

carpet noun (plural **carpets**) a covering for a floor, made of heavy fabric.

carrot noun (plural **carrots**) a long, orange vegetable that comes to a point at one end.

carry verb (**carries; carrying; carried**) hold something and move with it: He was carrying a suitcase.

cart noun (plural **carts**) a wooden vehicle for carrying things in, which can be pulled by a horse or a person.

carton noun (plural **cartons**) a cardboard or plastic container that holds food or a drink.

cartoon noun (plural **cartoons**) **1** a funny drawing in a newspaper or magazine. **2** a film made up of funny drawings.

cartridge noun (plural **cartridges**) a container of ink for using in a computer printer.

carve verb (**carves; carving; carved**) **1** make an object by cutting it out of wood, metal or stone: He carved a statue of a lion. **2** cut meat into slices.

case noun (plural **cases**) **1** a portable container for carrying objects in. **2** an instance of disease or discomfort: a case of the flu.

cash noun physical money.

castle noun (plural **castles**) a large, strong building with high stone walls to protect it from attack.

cat noun (plural **cats**) a furry animal with four legs and a tail, which people often keep as a pet.

catalog noun (plural **catalogs**) a list of the things that a company has for sale.

catch verb (**catches; catching; caught**) **1** get hold of something that is moving: I threw the ball and Anil caught it. **2** get on a bus or train to travel somewhere. **3** get an illness: I have caught a cold.

caterpillar noun (plural **caterpillars**) a small creature that looks like a worm, which will become a moth or a butterfly.

cattle noun cows and bulls.

cauliflower noun (plural **cauliflowers**) a large, rounded, white vegetable with green leaves on the outside.

cave noun (plural **caves**) a large hole in a cliff or hillside, or under the ground.

CD noun (plural **CDs**) a compact disc; a round, flat piece of plastic

that music, pictures, or computer information can be stored on.

ceiling noun (plural **ceilings**) the surface across the top of a room.

celebrate verb (**celebrates; celebrating; celebrated**) do something enjoyable because it is a special day: Mom and Dad are having a party to celebrate their wedding anniversary.

cell noun (plural **cells**) a small room where a prisoner is kept in a prison.

cellar noun (plural **cellars**) a room under a house, where things can be stored.

cement noun a powder that is mixed with water and sand and used to hold bricks together when building.

center noun (plural **centers**) **1** the middle of something. **2** a building that is used for particular activities: a sports center.

century noun (plural **centuries**) one hundred years.

cereal noun (plural **cereals**) **1** a plant, such as wheat or oats, that is grown for its seeds, which are called grain and are used for food. **2** a kind of food made from grain that is often eaten with milk for breakfast.

certain adjective very sure about something: I feel certain that it will rain today.

certificate noun (plural **certificates**) a piece of paper that proves that something important happened: a marriage certificate.

chair noun (plural **chairs**) a piece of furniture for one person to sit on.

chalk noun a stick of soft, white or colored rock, used for writing on a blackboard.

champion noun (plural **champions**) a person who has won a sporting contest: the world heavyweight boxing champion.

chain noun (plural **chains**) a line of metal rings joined together.

chance noun (plural **chances**) an opportunity to do something: We got the chance to go to the championship game.

change verb (**changes; changing; changed**) **1** become different: When the traffic lights change to red, you must stop. **2** make something different: She has changed the color of her hair. **3** put on different clothes: I changed into my pajamas.
+ noun (plural **changes**) **1** something that has become different: There's been a change in the weather. **2** money that a shopkeeper gives you back when you pay more than the price for something.

channel noun (plural **channels**) **1** a narrow passage for water. **2** a television station.

chapter noun (plural **chapters**) a section of a book.

character noun (plural **characters**) **1** a person in a story, film, or television program. **2** the kind of person you are: He is like his father in character.

charity noun (plural **charities**) an organization that raises money to help people in need.

charm noun (plural **charms**) **1** a small ornament that is attached to a bracelet. **2** in a story, special words that are said to cast a magic spell.

chart noun (plural **charts**) a piece of paper that shows dates, numbers or other information.

chase verb (**chases; chasing; chased**) run after someone or something and try to catch them.

chat verb (**chats; chatting; chatted**) talk to someone in a friendly way.

cheap adjective (**cheaper; cheapest**) not costing much money: cheap train fares.

cheat verb (**cheats; cheating; cheated**) do something dishonest or against the rules to try to get an advantage.

check verb (**checks; checking; checked**) look at something carefully to make sure it is all right.

+ noun (plural **checks**) a pattern of squares in different colors.

checkout noun (plural **checkouts**) the place in a store where you pay for the things you are buying.

cheek noun (plural **cheeks**) one of the two sides of your face below your eyes.

cheer verb (**cheers; cheering; cheered**) show you are pleased about something by shouting: The crowd cheered loudly when the band came on stage.

cheese noun a food made from milk, often having a strong taste.

cheetah noun (plural **cheetahs**) a large wild animal of the cat family with spotted fur.

chef noun (plural **chefs**) a person who cooks the food in a restaurant.

chemistry noun (plural **chemistries**) a science that studies and makes changes to matter, which is what makes up everything on Earth.

cherry noun (plural **cherries**) a small, round, soft fruit with red or purple skin.

chess noun a game for two people that is played on a board marked with black and white squares.

chest noun (plural **chests**) **1** the top part of the front of your body, between your neck and your stomach. **2** a large, strong, wooden box.

chew verb (**chews; chewing; chewed**) break food down with your teeth before you swallow it.

chicken noun (**plural chickens**) a bird that is kept on a farm for its eggs and meat.

chicken pox noun a children's illness that gives you red, itchy spots.

chief noun (plural **chiefs**) a person who is in charge of other people.

child noun (plural **children**) a boy or girl.

chimney noun (plural **chimneys**) a pipe that takes smoke from a fire out of a building, up into the air.

chimpanzee noun (plural **chimpanzees**) a small ape with black fur.

chin noun (plural **chins**) the bottom part of your face, below your mouth.

chip noun (plural **chips**) **1** a long, thin, piece of potato that has been fried. **2** a mark in something where a small piece has broken off. **3** a tiny piece of material that makes a computer work.

chocolate noun (plural **chocolates**) a sweet food made from cocoa, milk, and sugar.

choice noun (plural **choices**) **1** something that you choose: The red dress was my choice. **2** the things that you can choose from: There was a choice of milk, water, or orange juice.

choir noun (plural **choirs**) a large group of people who sing together.

choke verb (**chokes; choking; choked**) be unable to breathe properly.

choose verb (**chooses; choosing; chose; chosen**) decide which thing you want; pick something.

chop verb (**chops; chopping; chopped**) cut something up with an axe or a knife.
★ noun (plural **chops**) a thick slice of lamb or pork with a bone in it.

church noun (plural **churches**) a building where Christians go to worship God.

cinema noun (plural **cinemas**) a building where people go to watch films.

circle noun (plural **circles**) a round shape.

circus noun (plural **circuses**) a kind of entertainment which includes acrobats, clowns, and sometimes animal acts performing in a large tent.

city noun (plural **cities**) a large town.

clap verb (**claps; clapping; clapped**) hit your hands together so that they make a noise.

class noun (plural **classes**) a group of children who are taught together.

classroom noun (plural **classrooms**) a room in a school where a class is taught.

claw noun (plural **claws**) one of the sharp, curved nails on a bird's or animal's feet.

clay noun a kind of soft, sticky earth that becomes hard when it is dried and is used to make pots and bricks.

clean adjective (**cleaner; cleanest**) not dirty: a clean shirt.
+ verb (**cleans; cleaning; cleaned**) remove dirt from something.

clear adjective (**clearer; clearest**) **1** that can be seen through easily: clear water. **2** that can be understood easily: a clear explanation.

clever adjective (**cleverer; cleverest**) able to learn and understand things quickly.

click verb (**clicks; clicking; clicked**) make a short, sharp sound.

cliff noun (plural **cliffs**) a high, steep, hill made of rock.

climate noun (plural **climates**) the kind of weather that a place has.

climb verb (**climbs; climbing; climbed**) move upward, usually using your hands and feet.

cling verb (**clings; clinging; clung**) hold tightly onto someone or something: The little girl was clinging onto her mother.

clip noun (plural **clips**) a fastener that holds things together.
verb (**clips; clipping; clipped**) cut small pieces off something to shape it or make it neat.

cloakroom noun (plural **cloakrooms**) a room where people can hang up their coats.

clock noun (plural **clocks**) an instrument that shows the time.

close adjective (**closer; closest**) near to something: The hotel is close to the station.
+ verb (**closes; closing; closed**) shut something: Close the window!

cloth noun (plural **cloths**) material that is used to make clothes, etc.

clothes noun things that you wear, such as shirts, pants, and skirts.

cloud noun (plural **clouds**) a collection of white or gray mist that floats high in the sky.

clown noun (plural **clowns**) a performer in a circus who wears funny clothes and make-up and makes people laugh.

club noun (plural **clubs**) **1** an organization for people who share the same interest: the fishing club. **2** a thick, heavy stick used as a weapon.

clue noun (plural **clues**) something that helps you find the answer to a puzzle or mystery.

clumsy adjective (**clumsier; clumsiest**) awkward and careless in the way you move.

coach noun (plural **coaches**) a person who trains people in a particular skill: a singing coach.

coal noun a hard, black rock that comes from under the ground and is burned for heat.

coast noun (plural **coasts**) the edge of the land, next to the sea.

cobweb noun (plural **cobwebs**) a fine net that a spider makes to catch insects.

coat noun (plural **coats**) **1** a warm piece of clothing that you wear on top of your other clothes when you are outside. **2** the fur of an animal. **3** a layer of paint, etc.

cobra noun (plural **cobras**) a kind of large, venomous snake.

coconut noun (plural **coconuts**) a large fruit with a hard, brown shell and sweet, white flesh inside.

code noun (plural **codes**) a set of letters, numbers, or symbols that you use to send secret messages.

coffee noun a hot drink made from ground coffee beans.

coin see page 35.

cold adjective (**colder; coldest**) having a low temperature.
+ noun (plural **colds**) a common illness that

causes you to sneeze and cough and have a stuffy nose.

collar noun (plural **collars**) **1** the part of a shirt, blouse, or dress that folds over at the neck. **2** a leather band that goes around a dog's or cat's neck.

collect verb (**collects; collecting; collected**) **1** gather people or things together. **2** meet someone at a place and take them away: We collected the children from the party.

college noun (plural **colleges**) a place where some people go to study after they graduate from high school.

color noun (plural **colors**) the way something looks when light is shining on it: all the colors of the rainbow.

column noun (plural **columns**) **1** a thick, rounded, stone post that is part of a building. **2** a line of numbers or words written one below another.

coin

noun (plural **coins**) a piece of metal that is used as money.

US coins

British sterling coins

Australian coins

Euro-coins

comb noun (plural **combs**) a small piece of plastic or metal with fine teeth, which you use to adjust your hair.

comedy noun (plural **comedies**) a funny film or television program.

comfortable adjective easy to wear or to use: a comfortable chair.

comic noun (plural **comics**) a magazine that has stories told in pictures.

command verb (**commands; commanding; commanded**) order someone to do something.

common adjective (**commoner; commonest**) normal; not unusual: The pigeon is a common bird in the US.

company noun (plural **companies**) **1** an organization that makes and sells things: a toy company. **2** being with other people: Gran likes to have company on the weekend.

compare verb (**compares; comparing; compared**) look at people or things to see in what ways they are alike and in what ways they are different.

compass noun (plural **compasses**) an instrument that has a needle that always points north, which tells you which direction you are facing.

competition noun (plural **competitions**) a game or an event to find out who is best at doing something.

complain verb (**complains; complaining; complained**) say that you are not pleased with something: We complained to the waiter that our soup was cold.

complete adjective **1** all of something: a complete set of Roald Dahl books. **2** in every way; total: The party was a complete success. ✦ verb (**completes; completing; completed**) finish something: Have you completed your homework?

concentrate verb (**concentrates; concentrating; concentrated**) pay full attention to what you are doing: Concentrate on finishing your homework!

concerned adjective worried about something or someone: I'm concerned about Amy—she doesn't look well.

confident adjective feeling sure that you can do something or are good at something: I am confident that I will pass the test.

confuse verb (**confuses; confusing; confused**) **1** make someone feel unsure about what something means: I was confused by the instructions. **2** get two things or people mixed up in your mind: You are confusing me with my sister.

concert noun (plural **concerts**) a show in which people sing or play music.

confess verb (**confesses; confessing; confessed**) say that you have done something wrong: He confessed to stealing the money.

congratulate verb (**congratulates; congratulating; congratulated**) tell someone you are pleased about something special that has happened to them: I congratulated them on their engagement.

connect verb (**connects; connecting; connected**) join things together.

conscience noun a feeling of what is right and what is wrong.

conscious adjective awake and aware of what is going on around you: The patient is conscious again after his operation.

consider verb (**considers; considering; considered**)

computer noun (plural **computers**) an electronic machine that can store information and do calculations.

think carefully about something: He is considering changing his job.

container noun (plural **containers**) something, such as a box, cup, or bag, that you can put things in.

contents noun the things that are in something: She emptied the contents of her bag onto the desk.

contest noun (plural **contests**) a game or an event to find out who is best at doing something; a competition.

continent noun (plural **continents**) a very large area of land, such as Europe or Africa.

continue verb (**continues; continuing; continued**) go on doing something that you have been doing: We had a break and then continued working until five o'clock.

control verb (**controls; controlling; controlled**) make someone or something do what you want them to do.

conversation noun (plural **conversations**) talking to someone: We had an interesting conversation.

convince verb (**convinces; convincing; convinced**) make someone believe that what you are saying is true.

cook verb (**cooks; cooking; cooked**) make food fit to eat by heating it.

cool adjective (**cooler; coolest**) slightly cold.

copper noun a shiny, reddish-brown metal.

copy verb (**copies; copying; copied**) **1** do the same as someone else. **2** make something that is exactly the same as something else: Katie copied Shereen's homework. + noun (plural **copies**) something that is made to be exactly the same as something else: a copy of a famous painting.

coral noun a hard substance that is made from the bodies of tiny sea creatures.

cord noun (plural **cords**) a strong, thick string.

core noun (plural **cores**) the hard part in the center of a fruit such as an apple or pear.

cork noun (plural **corks**) a piece of bark from a tree called a cork oak tree that is used to close a bottle of wine, etc.

corn noun a tall plant grown for its large ears of starchy yellow or white grain, used as food.

corner noun (plural **corners**) the place where two edges or two streets meet.

correct adjective containing no mistakes; right. + verb (**corrects; correcting; corrected**) make right the mistakes in something.

corridor noun (plural **corridors**) a long passageway in a building with rooms leading off it.

cost verb (**costs; costing; cost**) be for sale for a certain amount of money: It costs a lot of money to buy a car.

costume noun (plural **costumes**) the clothes that an actor wears on stage or in a film or television program.

cot noun (plural **cots**) a baby's bed with bars on the sides.

cottage noun (plural **cottages**) a small house in the country.

cotton noun **1** a kind of cloth made from the fibers of the cotton plant. **2** a kind of thread made from cotton, which is used for sewing.

cough verb (**coughs; coughing; coughed**) force air from your lungs out of your mouth with a rough sound.

council noun (plural **councils**) a group of people who are chosen to make laws or give advice.

count verb (**counts; counting; counted**) **1** say numbers in order: I can count up to 10 in French. **2** work out how many of something there are: We counted all the children on the bus to make sure no one went missing.

counter noun (plural **counters**) **1** a narrow, flat surface where you are served in a shop, bank, etc. **2** a small piece of plastic that is used in some board games.

country noun (plural **countries**) **1** an area of land that has its own people and laws: Canada is a very large country. **2** land that is not in towns or cities: We went for a long walk in the country.

couple noun (plural **couples**) **1** two people who are married or having a romantic relationship. **2** two things or people: a couple of magazines.

coupon noun (plural **coupons**) a piece of printed paper that you can use to pay less than the full price for something.

courage noun willingness to do things that are dangerous or frightening.

course noun (plural **courses**) **1** a set of lessons. **2** a piece of ground for playing golf or running races.

court noun (plural **courts**) **1** a building where it is decided whether someone has committed a crime. **2** a piece of ground that is marked out for people to play tennis, squash, badminton, etc.

cousin noun (plural **cousins**) the son or daughter of your aunt or uncle.

cover verb (**covers; covering; covered**) put something over something else: Cover your mouth when you cough. noun (plural **covers**) something that goes over something else: She changed the covers on the bed.

cow noun (plural **cows**) a large animal that is kept on a farm for its milk and meat.

coward noun (plural **cowards**) a person who is not willing to do things that are dangerous or difficult.

1 a split that has developed in something without breaking into pieces. **2** a sudden, loud noise: the sharp crack of a gun.

cowboy noun (plural **cowboys**) a man who looks after cattle or horses or performs at a rodeo.

cozy adjective (**cozier; coziest**) warm and comfortable.

crab noun (plural **crabs**) a sea animal with a hard shell on its back.

crack verb (**cracks; cracking; cracked**) split without breaking into pieces: The windscreen cracked when a stone hit it.
+ noun (plural **cracks**)

cracker noun (plural **crackers**) **1** a thin, crisp bread product, sometimes eaten with cheese. **2** a colorful cardboard tube with a small toy inside, which makes a sudden, loud noise when people pull it apart.

cradle noun (plural **cradles**) a small bed for a very young baby, which can be rocked.

crane noun (plural **cranes**) a large machine that is used for lifting heavy objects.

crash noun (plural **crashes**) **1** an accident in which a vehicle bumps into something: a car crash. **2** the sudden, loud noise of something falling or crashing: Tim fell down the stairs with a crash.
+ verb (**crashes; crashing; crashed**) to bump into something with a sudden, loud noise.

crawl verb (**crawls; crawling; crawled**) move along on your hands and knees.

crayon noun (plural **crayons**) a colored pencil or stick of colored wax, used for drawing.

cream noun a thick, whitish liquid that rises to the top of milk.
+ adjective pale yellowish-white.

create verb (**creates; creating; created**) make or design something: The artist created a model of an eagle.

creature noun (plural **creatures**) any living thing.

creep verb (**creeps; creeping; crept**) move somewhere very quietly and slowly.

cricket noun (plural **crickets**) **1** a jumping insect that makes a chirping sound. **2** a team game in which players hit a ball with a bat and try to score points by running between two wickets.

crime noun (plural **crimes**) something that someone does which is against the law: Murder is a very serious crime.

criminal noun (plural **criminals**) a person who has done something that is against the law.

crisp adjective (**crisper; crispest**) **1** dry and easily broken. **2** pleasantly firm and fresh: the celery was crisp.

criticize verb (**criticizes; criticizing; criticized**) say what you think is wrong with someone or something.

crocodile noun (plural **crocodiles**) a large animal with a long body, short legs, scales, and very sharp teeth, which lives in water.

crooked adjective not straight: The picture is crooked.

cross adjective (**crosser; crossest**) angry or annoyed.
+ noun (plural **crosses**) two straight lines that cross each other.
+ verb (**crosses; crossing; crossed**) go across a road, etc.

crossword noun (plural **crosswords**) a word puzzle in which you write the answers to clues in small squares within a larger square.

crow noun (plural **crows**) a large black bird with a harsh cry.

crowd noun (plural **crowds**) a large number of people.

crown noun (plural **crowns**) a kind of hat made of gold or silver with jewels in it, which a king or queen wears.

cruel adjective (**crueler; cruelest**) very unkind and hurtful.

crumb noun (plural **crumbs**) a tiny piece of food such as bread or cake.

crumple verb (**crumples; crumpling; crumpled**) crush cloth or paper so that it becomes wrinkled.

crunch verb (**crunches; crunching; crunched**) bite or chew food noisily.

crush verb (**crushes; crushing; crushed**) damage something by pressing it hard.

crust noun (plural **crusts**) the hard part on the outside of a loaf of bread.

cry verb (**cries; crying; cried**) have tears coming out of your eyes, often because you are sad. + noun (plural **cries**) a sudden, loud sound; a shout.

cub noun (plural **cubs**) a young fox, wolf, bear, etc.

cube noun (plural **cubes**) a shape that has six square sides that are all the same size.

cuckoo noun (plural **cuckoos**) a bird that lays its eggs in other birds' nests.

cucumber noun (plural **cucumbers**) a long, green vegetable, often eaten raw in salads.

cuddle verb (**cuddles; cuddling; cuddled**) put your arms around someone and hold them close.

culprit noun (plural **culprits**) a person who has done something wrong.

cunning adjective clever and sly.

cup noun (plural **cups**) **1** a small container with a handle, which you drink from. **2** a silver cup given as a prize for winning a game or competition.

cupboard noun (plural **cupboards**) a piece of furniture with doors and sometimes shelves, which is used for storing things.

cure verb (**cures; curing; cured**) make someone well again when they have been ill.

curious adjective **1** interested to find out information. **2** strange or unusual.

curl noun (plural **curls**) a curved piece of hair.

curry noun (plural **curries**) a dish or sauce in Indian cooking seasoned with a mixture of spices.

cursor noun (plural **cursors**) a small mark that shows your position on a computer screen.

curtain noun (plural **curtains**) a large piece of cloth that hangs in front of a window and which you can pull across to cover the window.

curve noun (plural **curves**) a line that is bent rather than straight.

cushion noun (plural **cushions**) a kind of pillow that you sit on or lean against on a chair or sofa.

customer noun (plural **customers**) a person who buys something from a shop or another company.

cut verb (**cuts; cutting; cut**) **1** divide something into pieces with a knife or scissors. **2** injure yourself by breaking your skin on something sharp. noun (plural **cuts**) an injury caused by breaking your skin on something sharp.

cutlery noun knives, forks and spoons.

cycle noun (plural **cycles**) **1** a repeated series of events or actions. **2** a bicycle. verb (**cycles; cycling; cycled**) ride a bicycle.

cymbals noun a musical instrument consisting of two round pieces of metal that you bang together.

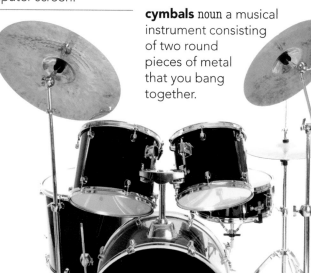

Dd

dad noun (plural **dads**) your father.

damp adjective (**damper; dampest**) slightly wet: a damp cloth.

daffodil noun (plural **daffodils**) a yellow flower that blooms in the spring.

dagger noun (plural **daggers**) a sharp pointed knife used as a weapon.

daisy noun (plural **daisies**) a small wildflower with white petals.

damage verb (**damages; damaging; damaged**) cause something to be harmed: The building was damaged by fire.

dangerous adjective likely to cause harm: a dangerous situation.

dare verb (**dares; daring; dared**) **1** be bold enough to do something: I wouldn't dare talk back to my parents. **2** challenge someone to do something risky or frightening: I dare you to ring the doorbell and run away.

dark adjective (**darker; darkest**) **1** having no light or hardly any light: a dark room. **2** (of a color) nearly black: dark brown.

dance verb (**dances; dancing; danced**) move in time to music.

data noun information about something; details.

date noun (plural **dates**) **1** the day, month, and year. **2** a soft, sticky brown fruit that grows on a palm tree.

daughter noun (plural **daughters**) a female child.

dawn noun the time of day when the sun rises in the sky and it begins to get light.

dead adjective no longer alive.

deaf adjective (**deafer; deafest**) unable to hear.

dear adjective (**dearer; dearest**) **1** that you care a lot about: a dear friend. **2** costing a lot of money.

decide verb (**decides; deciding; decided**) make up your mind about something: I decided to join the sports team.

deck noun (plural **decks**) one of the floors in a boat or a bus: We sat on the top deck.

decorate verb (**decorates; decorating; decorated**) **1** make something look attractive by adding things: We decorated the tree with colored lights. **2** make a room look nice with paint and wallpaper.

decrease verb (**decreases; decreasing; decreased**) become smaller in size or number: The number of children in the class has decreased.

deep adjective (**deeper; deepest**) that goes a long way down: a deep pool.

deer noun (plural **deer**) an animal that eats grass and has hooves and, in the male, large horns that are called antlers.

defeat verb (**defeats; defeating; defeated**) beat a person, a team, or an army: Paul beat Mark in a swimming race.

defend verb (**defends; defending; defended**) protect a person or a place from danger: The army defended the city from enemy attack.

definite adjective certain and not likely to change: a definite decision.

delete verb (**deletes; deleting; deleted**) remove something you have written or something you have keyed in a computer: I made a mistake, so I deleted it.

delicious adjective that tastes very good: a delicious cake.

delighted adjective very pleased or happy: I am delighted to see you.

deliver verb (**delivers; delivering; delivered**) take something to a place and hand it over to someone.

demonstrate verb (**demonstrates; demonstrating; demonstrated**) show someone how to do something.

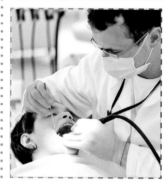

dentist noun (plural **dentists**) a person who takes care of your teeth.

depend verb (**depends; depending; depended**) **1** need someone to help you: The old lady depends on a friend to do her shopping. **2** be able to trust someone: I know I can depend on you to be quiet.

depth noun (plural **depths**) a measure of how deep something is.

describe verb (**describes; describing; described**) say what someone or something is like: She described Rachel as kind and pretty.

desert noun (plural **deserts**) a very dry place with very few plants.

deserve verb (**deserves; deserving; deserved**) have earned something good or something bad that you get by the way you have behaved: Ben deserves to win the prize because he has worked hard.

design verb (**designs; designing; designed**) draw a plan of the way something will look: The bride designed her own wedding dress.

desk noun (plural **desks**) a kind of table with drawers, where you can read and write.

dessert noun (plural **desserts**) something sweet that you eat at the end of a meal.

destroy verb (**destroys**; **destroying**; **destroyed**) completely ruin something: The flood has destroyed many homes.

detail noun (plural **details**) a small piece of information about something: The police officer wrote down all the details of the crime.

diamond noun (plural **diamonds**) **1** a very valuable, hard, clear-colored jewel. **2** a shape with four short sides of equal length and no right angles.

dice noun (plural **dice**) a small object that has six sides, each marked with a number of dots from one to six, which is used in some board games.

dictionary noun (plural **dictionaries**) a book that lists the words of a language in alphabetical order, with their meanings explained.

die verb (**dies**; **dying**; **died**) stop living.

diet noun (plural **diets**) **1** the kind of food that a person normally eats: Your diet should include lots of fruit.

2 the kind of food that a person eats if they want to become thinner or if they have a health problem: I need to go on a diet.

different adjective not the same as someone or something else: Cats are different from dogs.

difficult adjective that cannot be done easily: a difficult job.

dig verb (**digs**; **digging**; **dug**) make a hole in the ground with a shovel.

digital adjective **1** (of a clock or watch) that shows the time in figures rather than by a dial and hands. **2** that stores and sends information using the figures 0 and 1: a digital camera.

dim adjective (**dimmer**; **dimmest**) not bright: a dim light.

dinner noun (plural **dinners**) the main meal of the day.

dinosaur noun (plural **dinosaurs**) a very large lizard-like animal that lived on Earth millions of years ago.

dip verb (**dips**; **dipping**; **dipped**) put something into a liquid and take it back out quickly: I dipped my toes in the water.

direction noun (plural **directions**) the way in which someone or something is going or is facing: We walked in the direction of the church.

diary noun (plural **diaries**) a book in which you write about the events of the day or about your thoughts.

dirty adjective (**dirtier; dirtiest**) covered in mud or dust; not clean: Your hands are dirty.

disabled adjective (of a person) unable to do certain things because of an injury or condition affecting part of their body.

disagree verb (**disagrees; disagreeing; disagreed**) think differently from someone else about something: The two girls disagreed about which film to see.

disappear verb (**disappears; disappearing; disappeared**) go out of sight.

disappointed adjective feeling unhappy because something is not as good as you had expected it to be: We were disappointed with the show.

disaster noun (plural **disasters**) something terrible that happens, causing a lot of damage and sometimes death.

disc noun (plural **discs**) a round flat object.

discover verb (**discovers; discovering; discovered**) find something or find out about something.

discuss verb (**discusses; discussing; discussed**) talk about something with another person: The men were discussing the football game.

disease noun (plural **diseases**) an illness.

disguise noun (plural **disguises**) a set of clothes that change your appearance so that people will not recognize you.

disgusting adjective extremely unpleasant: a disgusting smell.

dish noun (plural **dishes**) a plate or bowl that holds food.

dislike verb (**dislikes; disliking; disliked**) not like someone or something: Sam dislikes broccoli.

display noun (plural **displays**) an exhibition of something: a fireworks display.

distance noun a measure of how far two places are from each other.

district noun (plural **districts**) a part of a town, city, or country: the only school in the district.

disturb verb (**disturbs; disturbing; disturbed**) interrupt someone while they are doing something or while they are enjoying a peaceful time: Don't disturb your father while he is sleeping.

dive verb (**dives; diving; dived**) jump into water head first.

divide verb (**divides; dividing; divided**) 1 split something up into smaller parts: Divide the chocolate bar in two. 2 in mathematics, figure out how many times one number fits into another, larger number: Ten divided by two is five.

divorce noun (plural **divorces**) the ending of a marriage.

doctor noun (plural **doctors**) a person who treats people who are ill and helps them get better.

document noun (plural **documents**) 1 a piece of paper with important information on it. 2 in a computer, pieces of information that you have written and stored together as a file.

domino noun (plural **dominoes**) a small, flat, black block of plastic or wood marked with different numbers of spots, used in playing a game called dominoes.

dog noun (plural **dogs**) a furry animal with four legs and a tail, which barks and which people often keep as a pet.

doll noun (plural **dolls**) a children's toy in the shape of a small person.

dollar noun (plural **dollars**) a unit of money that is used in the USA and some other countries.

dolphin noun (plural **dolphins**) an animal that lives in the ocean and looks like a large fish.

donkey noun (plural **donkeys**) an animal that looks like a small horse, but with longer ears.

door noun (plural **doors**) a large piece of wood or glass fixed into a wall, which you open to go into or go out of a room or building.

dot noun (plural **dots**) a tiny spot or mark.

double adjective twice as big or twice as many: a double bed.

doubt noun (plural **doubts**) a feeling of not being sure about something.

dozen noun (plural **dozens**) twelve: a dozen eggs.

draft noun (plural **drafts**) **1** cold air blowing into a room. **2** a version of something written or drawn that has or will have another version: the rough draft of my essay.

dragon noun (plural **dragons**) in stories, a creature like a huge lizard with wings that breathes fire.

drama noun (plural **dramas**) plays or acting: Jennifer takes classes in drama.

draw verb (**draws; drawing; drew; drawn**) **1** make a picture using a pencil or crayon. **2** open or close curtains by pulling them. **3** have an equal score at the end of a game or contest: The game was a draw with a score of 2–2.

drawer noun (plural **drawers**) a box in a piece of furniture that you open by sliding it out, which you can keep things in.

drawing noun (plural **drawings**) a picture made using a pencil, marker, or crayon: she made a drawing of her family.

dream verb (**dreams;**

dreaming; dreamed or **dreamt) 1** see things happening in your mind while you are asleep: I dreamed I was being chased by a monster last night. **2** think about something that you would very much like to happen: Julia dreams of becoming a model.

dress verb **(dresses;**

dressing; dressed) put on clothes.

+ noun (plural **dresses)** a piece of clothing with a skirt and top joined together, which girls and women wear.

drip verb **(drips; dripping;**

dripped) (of water) fall slowly in small drops.

drive verb **(drives;**

driving; drove; driven) make a vehicle move and control it.

drop verb **(drops;**

drink verb **(drinks; drinking; drank; drunk)** take a liquid into your mouth and swallow it.

+ noun (plural **drinks)** a liquid that you put in your mouth and swallow.

dropping; dropped) let something fall from your hands: He dropped the ball.

+ noun (plural **drops)** a very small amount of liquid.

drown verb **(drowns; drowning; drowned)** die because you are under water and unable to breathe.

drug noun (plural **drugs) 1** a medicine that you take to make you better when you are ill. **2** an illegal substance that some people take because they like the way it makes them feel, but which can be dangerous.

drum noun (plural **drums)**

a musical instrument that you play by beating it with sticks or with your hands.

dry adjective **(drier** or **dryer; driest** or **dryest)** not wet: a dry towel.

+ verb **(dries; drying; dried)** remove the water from something.

duck noun (plural **ducks)** a

bird that has webbed feet for swimming.

dull adjective **(duller;**

dullest) 1 not interesting; boring: a very dull story. **2** not bright or light: The weather was dull.

dusk noun the time of day when the sun sets and it begins to get dark.

dust noun dry, powdery dirt.

duty noun (plural **duties)** something that you have to do or that you feel you should do.

duvet noun (plural **duvets)**

a thick, light cover for a bed.

DVD noun (plural **DVDs)** a round flat disc that has sound and images recorded on it, which you can play in a machine.

dye verb **(dyes; dyeing; dyed)** change the color of something: She dyed her hair black.

Ee

eager adjective interest in doing something or having something: We were eager to get home.

early adverb **(earlier; earliest) 1** before the usual time: I got to school early. **2** near the beginning of the day or of another period of time: early in the morning.

earn verb **(earns; earning; earned)** get money by working for it: Andrew earns money by delivering newspapers.

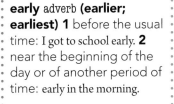

earring noun **(plural earrings)** a piece of jewelry that you wear in your ear.

eagle noun **(plural eagles)** a very large bird that eats smaller birds and animals.

earth noun **1** the planet where we live: the largest country on earth. **2** the soil in a garden, where plants grow: a pile of earth.

earthquake noun **(plural earthquakes)** a shaking of the ground, which can cause a lot of damage to buildings and people.

east noun one of the four main points of the compass, the direction where the sun rises.

easy adjective **(easier; easiest)** that you can do without any great difficulty: an easy problem.

eat verb **(eats; eating; ate; eaten)** put food in your mouth, chew it, and swallow it.

echo noun **(plural echoes)** a sound that is repeated when it bounces off a surface.

eclipse noun **(plural eclipses)** a time when the sun is hidden by the moon.

edge noun **(plural edges)** the part along the outside of something: the edge of the desk.

education noun teaching at school or college.

effect noun **(plural effects)** a change that is the result of something that happens: Smoking can have a harmful effect on your health.

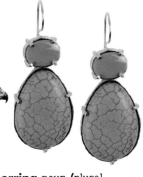

ear noun **(plural ears)** one of two parts on the sides of your head that you hear with.

effort noun (plural **efforts**) the energy that you use when you try hard to do something: He made an effort to finish his work.

electricity noun a kind of power that comes through wires, which produces light and makes machines work.

egg noun (plural **eggs**) an oval object that is laid by birds and some animals, which a baby bird or animal comes out of when it is being born.

elastic adjective able to stretch and go back into shape: an elastic band.

elbow noun (plural **elbows**) the joint in the middle of your arm, where it bends.

elephant noun (plural **elephants**) a very large gray animal with big ears and a long nose called a trunk.

email noun (plural **emails**) a message that you send from your computer to someone else's computer. verb (**emails; emailing; emailed**) send by email.

embarrassed adjective feeling shy or ashamed: She was embarrassed by all the attention.

emergency noun (plural **emergencies**) a sudden, very serious event.

employ verb (**employs; employing; employed**) give someone a job.

empty adjective (of a container, room, etc.) having nothing inside: an empty box.

encourage verb (**encourages; encouraging; encouraged**) tell someone that they should do something: My mother encouraged me to take piano lessons.

encyclopedia noun (plural **encyclopedias**) a large book that gives information on many different subjects.

end noun (plural **ends**) **1** the last part of something: the end of the film. **2** the farthest part of something: We walked to the end of the road. verb (**ends; ending; ended**) finish or stop: The party ends at five o'clock.

enemy noun (plural **enemies**) **1** a person who wants to harm you. **2** a country that fights against your country in a war.

energy noun **1** strength and liveliness. **2** the

power, such as electricity, that produces light and makes machines work.

engine noun (plural **engines**) the part of a vehicle that makes it move.

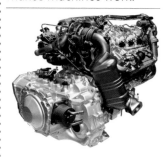

enjoy verb (**enjoys; enjoying; enjoyed**) get pleasure from doing something.

enormous adjective extremely large.

entertain verb (**entertains; entertaining; entertained**) amuse people.

enthusiastic adjective very keen and excited about something: enthusiastic about the concert.

entrance noun (plural **entrances**) the way into a building or other place.

envelope noun (plural **envelopes**) a folded paper container for a letter.

environment noun the world around us and the living things in it.

envy verb (**envies; envying; envied**) wish to have what someone else has.

episode noun (plural **episodes**) one part of a story that is shown on television in several parts.

equal adjective of the same size, number, or value as something else.

equator noun an imaginary line around the center of the earth.

equipment noun the things that you need to do something: gym equipment.

error noun (plural **errors**) a mistake.

erupt verb (**erupts; erupting; erupted**) (of a volcano) throw out hot ash and melted rocks.

escape verb (**escapes; escaping; escaped**) get away from a place or person.

even adjective **1** smooth and flat: an even surface. **2** (of a number) able to be divided by two.

evening noun (plural **evenings**) the part of the day between afternoon and night.

event noun (plural **events**) something important that happens.

evergreen adjective (of a tree) having leaves all year round.

evil adjective very bad, wicked.

exact adjective completely correct in every detail.

exaggerate verb (**exaggerates; exaggerating; exaggerated**) say that something is better, worse or bigger than it really is.

exam noun (plural **exams**) an important test that you take at school.

example noun (plural **examples**) something that shows what other things of its kind are like: This is an example of Grace's artwork.

excellent adjective extremely good: an excellent piece of work.

exchange verb (**exchanges; exchanging; exchanged**) give something to someone who gives you something else in its place: The girls exchanged magazines.

exciting adjective causing you to feel happy and lively; thrilling: an exciting ride at the fair.

excuse noun (plural **excuses**) a reason that someone gives for doing something wrong.

exercise noun (plural **exercises**) **1** movement, such as running and jumping, that you do to keep fit and healthy. **2** a piece of work that your teacher gives you to do: a spelling exercise.

exhausted adjective extremely tired.

exhibition noun (plural **exhibitions**) a show of pictures or other objects of interest that people can go to see.

exist verb (**exists; existing; existed**) live, be alive or present: Dinosaurs existed a very long time ago.

exit noun (plural **exits**) the way out of a building or other place.

expect verb (**expects; expecting; expected**) think that something is going to happen: I expect that Katie will win the race.

expensive adjective costing a lot of money.

experiment noun (plural **experiments**) a test to find out whether something works or whether something is true.

expert noun (plural **experts**) a person who is very good at something or who knows a lot about a subject: a computer expert.

explain verb (**explains; explaining; explained**) tell someone the meaning of something or the reason for something.

explode verb (**explodes; exploding; exploded**) burst with a loud bang.

explore verb (**explores; exploring; explored**) travel around a place to get to know it.

extinct adjective (of a kind of animal, etc.) that no longer exists: The dodo is an extinct bird.

extra adjective more than was expected or more than is needed.

extreme adjective very great: extreme heat.

eye noun (plural **eyes**) one of two parts in your face that you see with.

Ff

face noun (plural **faces**)
1 the front part of your head from the chin to the forehead.
2 the front, upper or outer surface of something: a clock face.
verb (**faces; facing; faced**)
1 turn your face toward: The house faces south. **2** meet and not avoid: He faced death bravely.

fact noun (plural **facts**) a piece of information that is real and true.

noun (plural **fairs**) a traveling entertainment with rides and stalls, especially one that comes to a place at the same time each year.

fairy noun (plural **fairies**) in a story, a small being with magic powers.

factory noun (plural **factories**) a building where machines make things.

fair adjective (**fairer; fairest**) **1** light in color: fair hair. **2** treating everyone equally.

fall verb (**falls; falling; fell; fallen**) **1** drop down toward the ground. **2** become less or lower in number. **3** (of the face) show sadness: His face fell at the news. **4** pass into a state that is mentioned: She fell asleep.

false adjective not true; not real: false teeth.

family noun (plural **families**) **1** a group of parents and their children; children of the same parents. **2** a group of related animals or plants: Dogs belong to the same family as foxes.

famine noun (plural **famines**) an extreme shortage of food.

famous adjective very well known and talked about a lot: a famous movie star.

fan noun (plural **fans**) **1** a machine that blows out cool air. **2** an enthusiastic supporter or admirer: a football fan.

fare noun (plural **fares**) the money you have to pay to make a journey in a train, bus, etc.

farm noun (plural **farms**) a piece of land and its buildings, used for growing crops or keeping animals.

fashion noun (plural **fashions**) a popular style, especially of clothes.

fast adjective (**faster; fastest**) **1** moving or able to move quickly. **2** (of a clock etc.) showing a time ahead of what is correct.
verb (**fasts; fasting; fasted**) go without all or some food for a certain time, especially because it is part of your religion.

fasten verb (**fastens; fastening; fastened**) fix firmly, especially by pinning, tying, or buttoning; make secure: Remember to fasten your seatbelt.

a b c d e f g h i j k l m n o p q r s t u v w x y z

fat adjective **(fatter; fattest)** having a big, round body.
noun an oily substance that comes from animals or plants and is used in cooking.

father noun (plural **fathers**) a male parent.

fault noun (plural **faults**) responsibility for doing something wrong: It was your fault that we missed the bus.

favorite adjective that you like best: Red is my favorite color.

fear noun (plural **fears**) feeling afraid or worried about something: Louise has a fear of spiders.

feather noun (plural **feathers**) one of the many soft, light pieces that make up the covering of a bird's body.

female adjective (of a person or animal) being a member of the sex that can have babies: A female horse is called a mare.

fence noun (plural **fences**) a barrier, usually made of wood, between one piece of land and another.

field noun (plural **fields**) a piece of land where a farmer grows crops or where grass grows.

fierce adjective **(fiercer; fiercest)** (of an animal) angry and dangerous.

fight verb **(fights; fighting; fought)** try to hurt someone by hitting and kicking them.

file noun (plural **files**) **1** a box or folder where you keep papers. **2** in a computer, pieces of information that are stored together and given a name. **3** a metal tool with a rough surface that is used to make rough things smooth.

film noun (plural **films**) a moving picture that tells a story, which you can watch at the movie theatre or on television.

final adjective last in a series: the final game of the season.

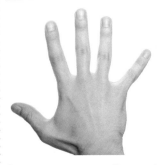

finger noun (plural **fingers**) one of the long parts that stick out from your hands, which you use to hold things and to pick things up.

finish verb **(finishes; finishing; finished)** bring something to an end, complete: Have you finished your homework?

fire noun (plural **fires**) **1** the flames produced when something is burning.
verb **(fires; firing; fire)** shoot a gun.

fire engine noun (plural **fire engines**) a large vehicle with equipment that firefighters use to put out fires.

firefighter noun (plural **firefighters**) a person whose job is to put out fires.

firework noun (plural **fireworks**) an object that makes pretty colors or patterns in the sky, and sometimes a loud noise, when you light it.

fish noun (plural **fish or fishes**) a creature with fins, scales, and a tail, which lives in the water.
verb **(fishes; fishing; fished)** try to catch fish.

fist noun (plural **fists**) a shape that you make with your hand when you curl your fingers around into your palm.

fit adjective (**fitter; fittest**) healthy and strong. verb (**fits, fitting, fitted**) be the right size for someone or something: This skirt fits me perfectly.

fix verb (**fixes; fixing; fixed**) **1** make right something that was broken, mend: My dad fixed my bike. **2** attach something securely to something else: The mirror is fixed to the wall.

flag noun (plural **flags**) a piece of fabric attached to a pole, which often represents a particular country.

flame noun (plural **flames**) a part of a fire that comes up into a point.

flash noun (plural **flashes**) a sudden, bright light that lasts for only a moment.

flat adjective (**flatter; flattest**) **1** smooth and even: a flat rock. **2** that does not have enough air inside: a flat tire. **3** lower than the true musical pitch.

flavor noun (plural **flavors**) (of food) taste.

flight noun (plural **flights**) **1** a journey by airplane. **2** the act of flying.

float verb (**floats; floating; floated**) stay on the surface of water without sinking.

flood noun (plural **floods**) a large amount of water covering the land: The heavy rain caused a flood.

floor noun (plural **floors**) **1** the part of a room that you walk on. **2** one of the levels of a tall building: We live on the tenth floor.

flour noun a powder made from crushed wheat, which is used for baking bread, cakes, etc.

flower noun (plural **flowers**) the part of a plant that has white or colored petals.

flu noun an illness that causes you to cough and sneeze, have a fever, and feel sore all over.

fly noun (plural **flies**) a small flying insect. verb (**flies; flying; flew; flown**) (of a bird, insect or airplane) travel through the air.

foam noun a lot of tiny air bubbles on top of a liquid.

fog noun a thick cloud made up of tiny drops of water that hangs in the air and makes it difficult to see.

folder noun (plural **folders**) **1** a cardboard container where you keep papers. **2** in a computer, a place where files can be stored together.

follow verb (**follows; following; followed**) go after someone or something: The teacher went first and the children followed her.

food noun things that you eat, which keep you healthy and give you energy.

foot noun (plural **feet**) one of two parts of your body that are on the end of your legs, and that you stand on.

football noun (plural **footballs**) **1** a game that is played between two teams who move the ball by kicking, passing, or running with it. **2** the ball that is used in the game of football.

force noun (plural **forces**) strength, power: The police opened the door by force. verb (**forces; forcing; forced**) make someone do something: The rain forced us to cancel the picnic.

foreign adjective from another country: foreign coins.

forest noun (plural **forests**) a large area of land with lots of trees growing close together.

forget verb (**forgets; forgetting; forgot; forgotten**) not remember something: I forgot to lock the door.

forgive verb (**forgives; forgiving; forgave; forgiven**) stop blaming someone for something wrong that they have done.

fork noun (plural **forks**) **1** a tool with prongs and a long handle that you use to eat with. **2** a place in a road where it splits into two roads that go in different directions.

fountain noun (plural **fountains**) a spray of water that goes up into the air, sometimes coming from a statue.

fox noun (plural **foxes**) a wild animal with reddish-brown fur that looks like a dog.

freckle noun (plural **freckles**) a small brown spot on the skin.

fruit

noun (plural **fruits** or **fruit**) the part of a plant that contains seeds and which usually can be eaten.

plum

coconut

pomegranate

banana

cherries

grapes

peach

mango

watermelon

apple

pear

strawberries

orange

pineapple

free adjective (**freer; freest**) **1** able to move about as you wish: The prisoners were set free. **2** that costs nothing: a free magazine.

fresh adjective (**fresher; freshest**) **1** (of food) newly produced: fresh vegetables. **2** (of water) not salty. **3** (of air) clean: A walk in the fresh air is good for you.

friend noun (plural **friends**) a person that you like very much and enjoy being with.

frighten verb (**frightens; frightening; frightened**) make someone feel afraid or worried.

frog noun (plural **frogs**) a small animal with smooth skin and long back legs that can live both on land and in water.

front noun (plural **fronts**) the part of something that faces forward.

frost noun (plural **frosts**) a light covering of tiny pieces of ice on the ground in very cold weather.

frown verb (**frowns; frowning; frowned**) have a serious facial expression because you are angry or worried.

frozen adjective **1** (of a lake or river) that has turned into ice. **2** (of food) stored in a very cold place, such as a freezer, so that it can be kept for a long time: frozen peas.

fruit see page 53.

full adjective unable to hold any more things or people: The box is full of books.

fun noun the happiness that you get from doing things that you enjoy.

funny adjective (**funnier; funniest**) **1** that makes you laugh: a funny story. **2** strange, unusual: a funny taste.

fur noun the soft hair that covers many animals' bodies.

furniture noun large objects such as chairs, tables, and bed.

future noun the time that is still yet to happen.

Gg

gale noun (plural **gales**) a strong wind.

gallery noun (plural **galleries**) a place where people can go to look at paintings or sculptures.

gallop verb (**gallops; galloping; galloped**) (of a horse) run fast.

game noun (plural **games**) an activity that you play for fun: a game of dominoes.

gang noun (plural **gangs**) a group of people who spend a lot of time together: I invited the gang over.

gap noun (plural **gaps**) a space between two things:

He has a gap between his two front teeth.

garage noun (plural **garages**) **1** a building where a car is kept. **2** a repair shop for cars.

garden noun (plural **gardens**) a piece of ground where flowers or vegetables are grown.

garlic noun an edible bulb shaped like an onion, which has a very strong taste and smell.

gas noun (plural **gases**) a substance that is neither a solid nor a liquid: Gas can be used for heating or cooking.

gate noun (plural **gates**) a kind of outside door in a wall or fence.

gaze verb (**gazes; gazing; gazed**) look steadily at someone or something for a long time.

gentle adjective (**gentler; gentlest**) kind and soft; not rough: She has a sweet, gentle nature.

genuine adjective real; not false: a genuine diamond ring.

geography noun a subject in which you learn about the earth and its countries, mountains, rivers, people, etc.

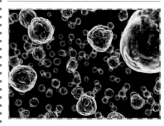

germ noun (plural **germs**) a tiny living thing that can make you sick if it gets into your body.

ghost noun (plural **ghosts**) the spirit of a dead person, which some people believe they can see.

a b c d e f g h i j k l m n o p q r s t u v w x y z

giant noun (plural **giants**) in fairy stories, an extremely large man.

gift noun (plural **gifts**) something that you give to someone to keep; a present.

gigantic adjective extremely large.

giggle verb (**giggles; giggling; giggled**) laugh in a silly way.

giraffe noun (plural **giraffes**) a very tall wild animal with long legs and an extremely long neck.

glad adjective (**gladder; gladdest**) very pleased and happy about something: I'm glad you could come to my party.

glass noun (plural **glasses**) 1 a clear, hard material that is easily broken, used to make windows and containers for drinks. 2 a container made of glass for holding drinks: a glass of water.

glasses noun a frame with two pieces of special glass in it, which people wear over their eyes to help them see more clearly.

glider noun (plural **gliders**) a kind of airplane with no engine, which moves along on a current of air.

glimpse noun (plural **glimpses**) a quick look at

something: I just caught a glimpse of the ocean between the buildings.

globe noun (plural **globes**) a ball-shaped model of the earth with a map of the world on it.

gloomy adjective (**gloomier; gloomiest**) 1 (of a place) dark and dull. 2 (of a person) feeling sad.

glove noun (plural **gloves**) a covering for the hand, which you wear to keep your hand warm: a pair of wool gloves.

glue noun a substance that you use to stick things together.

goal noun (plural **goals**) 1 in soccer, hockey, etc., the net that the players try to get the ball into to score a point. 2 in soccer, hockey, etc., a point scored by getting the ball into the net. 3 something that you aim to do some time: Her goal is to own her own business.

goat noun (plural **goats**) an animal with horns that is sometimes kept on a farm for its milk.

god noun (plural **gods**) a being that people worship.

gold noun a very valuable, shiny, yellowish metal.

goldfish noun (plural **goldfish**) a small orange-colored fish that people often keep as a pet.

golf noun a game in which you try to hit a small, hard ball into special holes with a long stick called a club.

good adjective (**better; best**) 1 (of a person) kind and nice. 2 pleasant or enjoyable: I had a good time at the party. 3 having a talent for doing something: Stewart is very good at drawing.

goose noun (plural **geese**) a bird with a long neck and webbed feet that can swim and is larger than a duck.

gorgeous adjective very pleasing to look at; beautiful: a gorgeous evening dress.

gorilla noun (plural **gorillas**) a very large ape with thick, black fur.

grab verb (**grabs; grabbing; grabbed**) take hold of something quickly and roughly.

graceful adjective moving in a smooth, beautiful way.

grain noun (plural **grains**) 1 the seeds of plants like wheat and oats, which are used for food. 2 a very small, hard piece of salt, sand, etc.

grandfather noun (plural **grandfathers**) your father's father or your mother's father.

grandmother noun (plural **grandmothers**) your father's mother or your mother's mother.

grape noun (plural **grapes**) a very small, soft fruit that grows in bunches and is sometimes used to make wine.

grapefruit noun (plural **grapefruits**) a large, round, juicy fruit with thick, yellow skin and a sour taste.

grass noun a very common green plant with long, thin leaves, which is used for lawns.

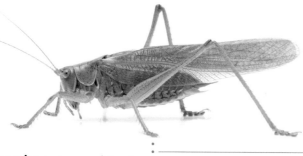

grasshopper noun (plural **grasshoppers**) a jumping insect that makes a chirping sound.

grateful adjective feeling thankful for something nice that someone has done for you: I am grateful to you for all your help.

green adjective (**greener; greenest**) of the color of grass.

grave noun (plural **graves**) a hole dug in the ground, where a dead body is buried.
adjective (**graver; gravest**) very serious and worrying: The soldiers are in grave danger.

gray adjective (**grayer; grayest**) of a color between black and white, like the sky on a dull day.

grease noun a soft, thick, oily substance.

great adjective (**greater; greatest**) 1 very large: a great oak tree. 2 (of a person) very clever or important: a great artist. 3 wonderful; very good: We had a great holiday.

greedy adjective (**greedier; greediest**) wanting more of something than you need.

greenhouse noun (plural **greenhouses**) a building with glass walls and a glass roof, used for growing plants in.

grin verb (**grins; grinning; grinned**) smile broadly.

grip verb (**grips; gripping; gripped**) hold something tightly: The child gripped her mother's hand.

groan verb (**groans; groaning; groaned**) make a low sound in your throat because you are in pain or are displeased about something.

growl verb (**growls; growling; growled**) make a low, rough, angry sound in the throat.

grown-up noun (plural **grown-ups**) a man or woman; an adult.

grunt verb (**grunts; grunting; grunted**) make a low, rough, angry sound in the throat.

guard verb (**guards; guarding; guarded**) watch a person or a place to make sure they are safe.
noun (plural **guards**) a person who watches a person or a place to make sure they are safe.

guess verb (**guesses; guessing; guessed**) try to answer a question without knowing if your answer is correct: I guessed it was about ten o'clock.

guest noun (plural **guests**) a person who is invited to a party or to stay at someone's house.

guide verb (**guides; guiding; guided**) lead someone to a place.
noun (plural **guides**) 1 a person who leads people to a place or shows people around a place. 2 a book that gives information about a place or a subject: a guide to the Greek Islands.

guilty adjective (**guiltier; guiltiest**) 1 having done something wrong: He was found guilty of murder. 2 having an unhappy feeling because you have done something wrong: I felt guilty for hurting her feelings.

guitar noun (plural **guitars**) a musical instrument that you play by pulling the strings with your fingers.

gum noun (plural **gums**) 1 one of the firm, pink parts of your mouth that your teeth are set into. 2 a soft candy that you chew without swallowing. 3 a sticky substance that comes from plants and is hard when it dries.

gun noun (plural **guns**) a weapon that fires bullets.

gym noun (plural **gyms**) a place with special equipment for doing exercises.

a b c d e f g h i j k l m n o p q r s t u v w x y z

Hh

habit noun (plural **habits**) something that you keep doing without thinking about it: Angie has a habit of biting her nails.

hail noun small balls of ice that fall from the sky.

hair noun **1** the mass of fine strands that grow on your head, or on other parts of a person's or animal's body: She wore her hair in a ponytail. **2** one of these strands: I found a hair in my soup.

hairdresser noun (plural **hairdressers**) a person whose job is to cut and style people's hair.

half noun (plural **halves**) one of two equal parts of something: The second half of the game was very exciting.

hall noun (plural **halls**) **1** a corridor with rooms leading off it. **2** a large room, where public events are held: The concert will be held in the main hall.

ham noun meat that comes from the leg of a pig, which has been smoked or salted.

hamburger noun (plural **hamburgers**) ground beef formed into a flat, round shape, which is grilled or fried and eaten in a bread roll.

hammer noun (plural **hammers**) a heavy tool that is used for hitting nails into wood or a wall.

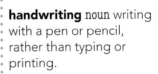

hand noun (plural **hands**) one of two parts of your body that are on the end of your arms.

handbag noun (plural **handbags**) a small bag that women carry with them to hold their cell phone, wallet, and other small items.

handkerchief noun (plural **handkerchiefs**) a small square of cloth that you use to wipe your face, nose, or eyes.

handle noun (plural **handles**) the part of a door, tool, etc., that you hold in your hand. verb (**handles; handling; handled**) feel or hold something with your hands: Handle the ornaments carefully.

handsome adjective (of a man) very pleasing to look at.

handstand noun (plural **handstands**) standing on your hands with your legs straight up in the air.

handwriting noun writing with a pen or pencil, rather than typing or printing.

hang verb (**hangs; hanging; hung**) put something on a hook, nail, etc., so that it is not touching the ground: Hang your coats up in the closet.

happen verb (**happens; happening; happened**) **1** take place: What happened at the party? **2** do something without planning to do it: I happened to meet Ravi in town.

happy adjective (**happier; happiest**) feeling pleased or glad; not sad: We are very happy in our new home.

harbor noun (plural **harbors**) a place where people can tie up boats and leave them safely.

hard adjective (**harder; hardest**) **1** solid and firm; not soft. **2** that cannot be done easily: a hard task.

hardly adverb only just; almost not: The bag was so heavy that I could hardly lift it.

hare noun (plural **hares**) an animal that looks like a large rabbit with longer ears and longer legs.

harm verb (**harms; harming; harmed**) damage or injure someone or something.

harvest noun (plural **harvests**) the time of year when farmers gather their crops.

hat noun (plural **hats**) something that you wear on your head.

hate verb (**hates; hating; hated**) dislike someone or something strongly.

haunted adjective (of a place) that some people believe is visited by a ghost: a haunted house.

hay noun dried grass for feeding to animals.

head noun (plural **heads**) **1** the part of your body on top of your neck, which contains your eyes, ears, nose, mouth, and brain. **2** the person who is in charge of an organization or a group: the head of the sales department.

headache noun (plural **headaches**) a pain in your head.

heading noun (plural **headings**) a title at the top of a piece of writing.

headline noun (plural **headlines**) the title at the top of a piece of writing in a newspaper, which is printed in large type.

headphones noun a pair of small speakers that you wear over your ears so that you can listen to recorded music without other people hearing it.

healthy adjective (**healthier; healthiest**) **1** (of a person) fit and well. **2** good for your health: a healthy diet.

heap noun (plural **heaps**) a pile of things one on top of another.

hear verb (**hears; hearing; heard**) notice a sound with your ears: I heard a dog barking.

heart noun (plural **hearts**) **1** the part of your body in

your chest that pumps the blood around your body. **2** a shape like a heart, representing love.

heat noun a hot feeling; warmth.
verb (**heats; heating; heated**) make something hot: Heat the milk and pour it onto the coffee.

heavy adjective (**heavier; heaviest**) weighing a lot.

hedge noun (plural **hedges**) a line of bushes that forms an edge to a garden or field.

hedgehog noun (plural **hedgehogs**) a small animal that is covered in spines.

heel noun (plural **heels**) **1** the back part of your foot. **2** the raised back part underneath a shoe.

height noun (plural **heights**) the measurement of how high or how tall a person or thing is.

helicopter noun (plural **helicopters**) a kind of aircraft with large blades on its roof that turn very quickly.

help verb (**helps; helping; helped**) do something that makes it easier for someone to do something: Will you help me to look for my glasses?

hero noun (plural **heroes**) **1** a man or woman who is much admired and respected, especially because they are very brave. **2** the main character in a book, film, or play.

heroine noun (plural **heroines**) **1** a woman who is much admired and respected, especially because she is very brave. **2** the main female character in a book, film or play.

hesitate verb (**hesitates; hesitating; hesitated**) pause before doing something.

hibernate verb (**hibernates; hibernating; hibernated**) (of an animal) spend the winter in a deep sleep.

hide verb (**hides; hiding; hid; hidden**) **1** go to a place where you cannot be seen. **2** put something in a place where it cannot be seen.

high adjective (**higher; highest**) **1** tall: a high tower. **2** being a long way above the ground: The sun was high in the sky.

hill noun (plural **hills**) a rounded area of high land.

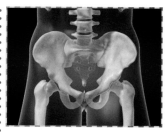

hip noun (plural **hips**) one of two parts of your body between your waist and your legs.

hippopotamus noun (plural **hippopotamuses** or **hippopotami**) a very large wild animal with thick skin and short legs, which spends most of its time in water.

hire verb (**hires; hiring; hired**) give work to someone in exchange for pay: The company hired new workers.

hiss verb (**hisses; hissing; hissed**) make a noise that sounds like "sss."

history noun a subject in which you learn about things that happened in the past.

hit verb (**hits; hitting; hit**) knock someone or something quickly and hard.

hoarse adjective (**hoarser; hoarsest**) (of a voice) that sounds rough; not clear.

hobby noun (plural **hobbies**) something that you do because you enjoy it or are interested in it: My hobby is collecting foreign coins.

a b c d e f g h i j k l m n o p q r s t u v w x y z

hole noun (plural **holes**) a space or gap in something: There's a hole in your sock.

holiday noun (plural **holidays**) a day of celebration on which schools and business are often closed.

hollow adjective having a space inside: a hollow chocolate egg.

home noun (plural **homes**) the place where you live.

homework noun school work that you do at home.

honest adjective truthful and trustworthy.

honey noun a soft, sweet, sticky food made by bees, which you can spread on bread.

hood noun (plural **hoods**) part of a coat or jacket that covers your head.

hoof noun (plural **hooves** or **hoofs**) the hard part of the foot of an animal such as a horse or a deer.

hook noun (plural **hooks**) a curved piece of metal for hanging things on or for catching fish with.

hoop noun (plural **hoops**) a large ring made of plastic, metal, or wood.

hop verb (**hops; hopping; hopped**) **1** (of a person) jump on one foot. **2** (of a bird) jump with both feet.

hope verb (**hopes; hoping; hoped**) want something to happen: I hope you will feel better soon.

horizon noun (plural **horizons**) the line in the distance where it looks as if the sky touches the ground or the sea.

horizontal adjective parallel to the ground.

horn noun (plural **horns**) **1** one of the hard, pointed parts on the head of an animal such as a goat. **2** a brass musical instrument that you play by blowing into it. **3** the part of a car that makes a loud noise as a warning.

horrible adjective very unpleasant or nasty.

horror noun a strong feeling of fear or shock.

horse noun (plural **horses**) a large animal that people can ride or that can pull a cart.

hose noun (plural **hoses**) a long tube attached to a tap, which sprays water.

hospital noun (plural **hospitals**) a place where sick or injured people go to be taken care of.

hot adjective (**hotter; hottest**) **1** of a high temperature; very warm. **2** (of food) having a strong, spicy taste.

hotel noun (plural **hotels**) a building where people can pay to stay for a while.

hour noun (plural **hours**) a period of 60 minutes.

house noun (plural **houses**) a building where people live.

howl verb (**howls; howling; howled**) (of an animal) to make a long, high-pitched cry.

hug verb (**hugs; hugging; hugged**) put your arms around someone and hold them close.

huge adjective (**huger; hugest**) very large.

hum verb (**hums; humming; hummed**) sing with your lips closed: Michelle was humming a happy tune.

human noun (plural **humans**) a man, woman, or child; a person.

humor noun the ability to make people laugh or to enjoy things that are funny: Daniel has a good sense of humor.

hump noun (plural humps) a large, rounded lump on a camel's back, where it stores fat and water.

hungry adjective (**hungrier; hungriest**) feeling the need to eat.

hunt verb (**hunts; hunting; hunted**) **1** chase an animal to kill it for food or as a sport. **2** search for something: I hunted all over the house for my phone.

hurricane noun (plural **hurricanes**) a storm with extremely strong winds.

hurry verb (**hurries; hurrying; hurried**) move very quickly; rush.

hurt verb **(hurts; hurting; hurt) 1** cause someone to feel pain; injure someone: Lisa was hurt in a car accident. **2** feel sore: My head hurts.

husband noun (plural **husbands)** a male partner in a marriage.

hut noun (plural **huts)** a small building, often made of wood.

hutch noun (plural **hutches)** a box made of wood and wire, where you keep a small pet such as a rabbit.

ice noun frozen water.

iceberg noun (plural **icebergs)** a huge block of ice in the ocean in a very cold climate.

ice cream noun a sweet, frozen dessert made from cream, sugar, and flavorings.

ice skate noun (plural **ice skates)** a boot with a metal blade fixed to the bottom, used for gliding on ice.

icicle noun (plural **icicles)** a long pointed piece of ice that hangs down from a place where water has been dripping.

icing noun a sweet topping for a cake, usually made from powdered sugar and water.

icy adjective **(icier; iciest) 1** covered in ice: icy roads. **2** extremely cold: an icy wind.

idea noun (plural **ideas)** a thought, plan or suggestion: That was a brilliant idea.

ideal adjective the best possible; perfect: This house is ideal for a family.

identical adjective exactly the same in every way.

idle adjective **(idler; idlest)** doing very little; lazy.

igloo noun (plural **igloos)** a small, rounded house made from blocks of hard snow.

ignore verb **(ignores; ignoring; ignored)** pay no attention to someone or something: Amy ignored my advice to take an umbrella.

ill adjective not feeling well.

illegal adjective against the law: It's illegal to drop litter in the street.

illustrate verb **(illustrates; illustrating; illustrated)** add pictures to a book, etc.

imitate verb **(imitates; imitating; imitated)** copy what someone does, especially the way they speak.

immediately adverb right away.

impatient adjective not liking to be kept waiting.

important adjective **1** (of a thing) that matters a lot: I have important news for you. **2** (of a person) having a lot of power.

impossible adjective that cannot be done: an impossible task.

impress verb **(impresses; impressing; impressed)** make someone think well of you: His eagerness to help really impressed me.

improve verb **(improves; improving; improved) 1** make something better: You must improve your handwriting. **2** get better: Jamil's reading has improved.

include verb **(includes; including; included)** make something a part of something else: All meals are included in the price.

increase verb **(increases; increasing; increased)** become larger in size or number.

independent adjective able to do things by yourself; not depending on other people to do things for you.

index noun (plural **indexes)** a list in alphabetical order at the back of a book of people or things of interest that are mentioned in the book.

individual adjective that is for one person, rather than a whole group: an individual pizza.

infant noun (plural **infants)** a very young child.

influence verb **(influences; influencing; influenced)** have an important effect on the way someone thinks or behaves.

information noun facts about something: I'm looking for information on Australia.

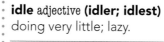

60

ingredient noun (plural **ingredients**) one of the things that are used to make something: The ingredients needed to make a cake are flour, sugar, butter, and eggs.

inhabitant noun (plural **inhabitants**) a person who lives in a particular place: The town has 10,000 inhabitants.

initial noun (plural **initials**) the first letter of a word or name.

injection noun (plural **injections**) putting medicine into someone's body using a special needle.

injure verb (**injures; injuring; injured**) hurt someone: She was badly injured in the accident.

ink noun the black or colored liquid that is used for writing and printing.

innocent adjective (of a person) having done nothing wrong.

insect noun (plural **insects**) a small creature with six legs and sometimes wings.

insist verb (**insists; insisting; insisted**) say something firmly: I insist that you let me buy the tickets.

inspect verb (**inspects; inspecting; inspected**) have a very close look at something; examine something.

instant adjective happening immediately: an instant success.

instinct noun (plural **instincts**) something that you do naturally, without learning it and without thinking about it.

instruction noun (plural **instructions**) information on how to do something: Follow the instructions on the packet.

instrument noun (plural **instruments**) **1** a tool that is used to do a particular job: surgical instruments. **2** see page 62.

insult verb (**insults; insulting; insulted**) upset someone by saying something rude or nasty about them.

intelligent adjective able to learn and understand things quickly.

intend verb (**intends; intending; intended**) plan to do something; do something deliberately: I didn't intend to upset you.

interesting adjective that makes you want to know about it or do it: an interesting story.

interfere verb (**interferes; interfering; interfered**) get involved in something that is not your business: Don't interfere in other people's arguments.

Internet noun a system by which people all over the world can communicate with each other by computer.

interrupt verb (**interrupts; interrupting; interrupted**) start talking while someone else is already talking: Don't interrupt me when I'm talking.

interview verb (**interviews; interviewing; interviewed**) try to learn about someone by asking them questions about themselves: The manager is interviewing people for the position of personal assistant.

introduce verb (**introduces; introducing; introduced**) let people meet each other for the first time: He introduced his new girlfriend to his parents.

introduction noun (plural **introductions**) a short part at the beginning of a piece of writing, explaining what it is about.

invent verb (**invents; inventing; invented**) create something that has never been made before.

investigate verb (**investigates; investigating; investigated**) examine something carefully to try to find out all the facts about it.

invisible adjective that cannot be seen.

invite verb (**invites; inviting; invited**) ask someone to come to your house or to go somewhere with you: Megan has invited me to her party.

involve verb (**involves; involving; involved**) include or affect someone or something: This is a matter that involves the whole family.

iPod noun (plural **iPods**) a small electronic machine on which you can listen to music that you have downloaded from the Internet.

iron noun (plural **irons**) **1** a strong, heavy metal, from which steel is made. **2** a piece of electrical equipment that is heated and used to smooth the creases out of clothes that have been washed and dried.

irritate verb (**irritates; irritating; irritated**) annoy someone.

island noun (plural **islands**) an area of land completely surrounded by water.

italics noun letters that are printed so that they are sloping.

itch verb (**itches; itching; itched**) cause a feeling in your skin that makes you want to scratch it: The mosquito bite on my leg is itching.

ivy noun a kind of plant that grows over walls.

instrument 2

something that you play music with, often by blowing into it, strumming its strings, pressing its keys, shaking it, or tapping on it.

accordion

tamborine

indian tabla drums

piano

banjo

mandolin

saxophone

mexican maracas

harmonica

acoustic guitar

carved african djembe

ocarina

flute

drums

violin

thumb piano

clarinet

Jj

jealous adjective annoyed because other people have what you would like to have.

jeans noun casual pants made of a strong cotton material called denim.

jelly noun a clear, soft, springy, sweet food made with fruit juice.

jacket noun (plural **jackets**) a short coat.

jail noun (plural **jails**) a place where criminals are locked up; a prison.

jet noun (plural **jets**) **1** a strong, thin stream of water that shoots upwards. **2** a very fast airplane.

jam noun **1** a soft, sticky food made from fruit and sugar, which you can spread on bread. **2** a situation in which there are so many vehicles in a place that they cannot move or can only move very slowly: We got stuck in a traffic jam.
verb (**jams; jamming; jammed**) get stuck in a certain position and be unable to be moved: The door is jammed.

jewelry noun ornaments that people can wear, such as necklaces, bracelets, and earrings.

jigsaw puzzle noun (plural **jigsaw puzzles**) a puzzle consisting of pieces of strong cardboard that make a picture when you put them together.

job noun (plural **jobs**) **1** the work that someone is paid to do: My mom has a job at the post office. **2** any task that has to be done: It's my job to feed the dog.

jog verb (**jogs; jogging; jogged**) **1** run at a slow pace: We jogged around the park. **2** knock or bump something: Jessie jogged my arm.

join verb (**joins; joining; joined**) **1** fasten or link things together: We stood in a circle and joined hands. **2** become a member of a club or an organization: I joined the Brownies last year.

joke noun (plural **jokes**) something funny that a person says or does to make people laugh.

journey noun (plural **journeys**) a trip, where you travel from one place to another: I was tired after a long train journey.

judge noun (plural **judges**) **1** the person who is in charge of a court of law and who has the power to decide how a guilty person should be punished. **2** a person who chooses the winner of a competition.
verb (**judges; judging; judged**) decide how good or bad something is.

judo noun a sport in which people fight each other with their hands and try to throw each other down onto the floor.

juggle verb (**juggles; juggling; juggled**) keep throwing objects in the air and catching them one at a time while keeping the others in the air.

juice noun a liquid that comes from fruit: a glass of orange juice.

jump verb (**jumps; jumping; jumped**) push yourself upward into the air: The children were jumping up and down excitedly.

K k

kangaroo noun (plural **kangaroos**) a large animal that lives in Australia, the female of which carries its baby in a pouch on the front of its body.

karate noun a sport in which people fight each other with their hands and feet.

kennel noun (plural **kennels**) a small wooden house for a dog.

ketchup noun a kind of thick, smooth sauce made from tomatoes.

key noun (plural **keys**) **1** a piece of metal that is shaped so that it fits into a lock, used to lock and unlock a door, etc. **2** one of the buttons that you press on a computer keyboard or a musical instrument such as a piano, in order to make it work.

keyboard noun (plural **keyboards**) a row of buttons called keys on a computer or on a musical instrument such as a piano, which you press to make it work.

kick verb (**kicks; kicking; kicked**) hit something or someone with your foot: Matthew kicked the ball over the fence.

kidnap verb (**kidnaps; kidnapping; kidnapped**) take someone away by force.

kill verb (**kills; killing, killed**) cause someone or something to die.

king noun (plural **kings**) a man who rules a country.

kiss verb (**kisses; kissing, kissed**) touch someone with your lips as a sign of affection.

kitchen noun (plural **kitchens**) a room where you cook food.

kite noun (plural **kites**) a light frame covered with paper or cloth, attached to a long piece of string, which you fly in the air while holding onto the end of the string.

kitten noun (plural **kittens**) a young cat.

kiwi fruit noun (plural **kiwi fruits**) a small fruit with a fuzzy, brownish skin and soft, green flesh.

knee noun (plural **knees**) the joint in the middle of your leg, which allows you to bend your leg.

kneel verb (**kneels; kneeling; kneeled** or **knelt**) sit with your knees and the bottom part of your legs touching the ground.

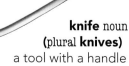

knife noun (plural **knives**) a tool with a handle and a sharp blade, used for cutting things.

knight noun (plural **knights**) a man who wore armor and rode into battle for his king or queen a very long time ago.

knit verb (**knits; knitting; knitted**) make clothes from yarn using two long needles.

knob noun (plural **knobs**) **1** a round handle on a door or drawer. **2** a round button on a machine, which you turn to make the machine work.

knot noun (plural **knots**) a tied piece of string or cloth.

knuckle noun (plural **knuckles**) one of the joints in your fingers where they bend.

koala noun (plural **koalas**) an animal with gray fur that lives in Australia, the female of which carries its baby in a pouch on the front of its body.

Ll

label noun (plural **labels**) a small piece of paper or cloth attached to something, with information written or printed on it.

lace noun (plural **laces**) **1** a kind of very fine cloth with a pattern of small holes. **2** a piece of cord in your shoe that you tie to fasten it.

ladder noun (plural **ladders**) a metal or wooden frame with steps, which you can climb to reach something high up.

ladybug noun (plural **ladybugs**) a small flying red insect with black spots.

lake noun (plural **lakes**) a large area of fresh water.

lamb noun (plural **lambs**) a young sheep.

lamp noun (plural **lamps**) a light that can be moved around, rather than being fixed to the ceiling of a room.

lane noun (plural **lanes**) **1** a small, narrow road. **2** a strip of a main road that is marked off from the rest of the road by painted lines so that one line of vehicles can use it.

language noun (plural **languages**) the words that the people from a particular country use when they speak or write.

laptop noun (plural **laptops**) a computer that you can easily carry around and that you can use while holding it on your knees rather than laying it on a desk or table.

large adjective (**larger; largest**) big: a large pizza for the whole family to share.

late adverb (**later; latest**) **1** after the usual or expected time: I arrived late for the concert. **2** near the end of the day or of another period of time: late in the evening.

laugh verb (**laughs; laughing; laughed**) make a sound with your voice that shows that you find something funny.

law noun (plural **laws**) a rule that is made by the government that everyone in the country has to obey.

lawn noun (plural **lawns**) an area of grass that is kept mowed short.

lay verb (**lays; laying; laid**) **1** put something in a certain position: lay a piece of paper on the table. **2** (of a female bird) produce an egg.

layer noun (plural **layers**) a single thickness of something: several layers of wallpaper.

lazy adjective (**lazier; laziest**) not willing to work or make an effort.

leader noun (plural **leaders**) the person who is in charge of a group of people.

leaf noun (plural **leaves**) one of the flat, green parts of a plant that grow out from the stems.

leaflet noun (plural **leaflets**) a piece of paper with information printed on it.

leak verb (**leaks; leaking; leaked**) (of a container) have a hole or a crack so that liquid comes out of it.

lean verb (**leans; leaning; leaned** or **leant**) **1** tilt in a particular direction: He leaned forward and gave her a hug. **2** rest your body against something: She was leaning against the wall. adjective (of meat) having no fat or very little fat.

leap verb (**leaps; leaping; leaped** or **leapt**) jump: He was leaping up and down.

learn verb (**learns; learning; learned** or **learnt**) find out about something: We are learning about ancient Egypt at school.

leather noun a material made from the skins of animals, used to make shoes, bags, etc.

left adjective of the side that is opposite from the right: I write with my left hand.

leg noun (plural **legs**) **1** one of two long parts of your body that start at your hips and end at your feet. **2** one of the parts of a piece of furniture that it rests on: the legs of the table.

lemon noun (plural **lemons**) a small, juicy fruit with yellow skin and a sour taste.

lend verb (**lends; lending; lent**) give something to someone for a while: Can you lend me an umbrella till tomorrow?

length noun (plural **lengths**) the measurement of how long something is.

leopard noun (plural **leopards**) a large wild animal of the cat family with spotted fur.

lesson noun (plural **lessons**) a short period of time when you are taught a subject: a history lesson.

letter noun (plural **letters**) **1** one of the symbols that are used to write words. **2** a message that you write and send to someone.

lettuce noun (plural **lettuces**) a large vegetable with green leaves that form a rounded shape, often eaten raw in salads.

level adjective smooth and flat: a level surface.

lever noun (plural **levers**) a handle that you pull down to make a machine work.

library noun (plural **libraries**) a place where you can go to read or borrow books.

lie verb **1** (**lies; lying; lay; lain**) rest with your body in a flat position: I was lying on the sofa. **2** (**lies; lying; lied**) say something that is not true.
  noun (plural **lies**) something you say that is not true.

life noun (plural **lives**) the time that someone is alive.

lifeboat noun (plural **lifeboats**) a boat that is used for rescuing people who are in danger at sea.

lift verb (**lifts; lifting; lifted**) move something upward: Lie on your back and lift your feet off the floor.
  noun (plural **lifts**) a machine that carries people from one floor in a building to another.

light noun (plural **lights**) something, such as a lamp, that gives out brightness.
  verb (**lights; lighting; lit**) **1** start a fire burning: Dad struck a match and lit the fire. **2** shine light in a place.
  adjective **1** (of a place) having plenty of light; bright: The room is nice and light. **2** (of a color) pale: light blue. **3** not weighing much: My bag is quite light.

lighthouse noun (plural **lighthouses**) a tower with a very bright light at the top, which guides ships to safety.

lightning noun a very bright flash of light that you see in the sky during a thunderstorm.

like verb (**likes; liking; liked**) be fond of someone or something: I like cats.
  preposition similar to someone or something: Dean looks like his father.

likely adjective (**likelier; likeliest**) probable: It's likely to be sunny tomorrow.

limb noun (plural **limbs**) an arm or a leg.

limit noun (plural **limits**) the point that you must not go beyond: The speed limit on this road is 30 miles per hour.

limp verb (**limps; limping; limped**) walk with uneven steps because you have a sore foot or leg.
  adjective (**limper; limpest**) soft; not stiff or firm: a limp lettuce leaf.

lion noun (plural **lions**) a large wild animal of the cat family with light brown fur.

lip noun (plural **lips**) one of the two soft edges of your mouth: I cut my bottom lip when I fell.

liquid noun (plural **liquids**) any substance, such as water, that is not a solid or a gas.

list noun (plural **lists**) a number of things that are written one below another.

listen verb (**listens; listening; listened**) pay attention to something that you can hear: Listen carefully to your teacher's instructions.

litter noun **1** trash that is dropped in the street. **2** a number of baby animals that are born to a mother animal at one time.

little adjective (**littler; littlest**) **1** small; not big: a little girl. **2** not much: I have very little money.

lizard noun (plural **lizards**) an animal with short legs, a long tail and scales on its body.

loaf noun (plural **loaves**) a large piece of bread that is cut into slices before being eaten.

lobster noun (plural **lobsters**) a sea animal with a hard shell on its back, eight legs, and two claws.

local adjective being near where you live: the local library.

lock noun (plural **locks**) the part on a door, window, etc., that you fasten and unfasten with a key.
  verb (**locks; locking; locked**) fasten a door, window, etc., by turning a key in a lock.

log noun (plural **logs**) a thick piece that has been chopped from the branch of a tree.

lonely adjective (**lonelier; loneliest**) feeling sad because you are alone.

long adjective (**longer; longest**) **1** measuring a lot in length: *a girl with long hair.* **2** lasting or taking up a lot of time: *a long film.*
verb (**longs; longing; longed**) want very much to have or do something: *I longed to go home.*

lord noun (plural **lords**) a person having power and authority over others.

lose verb (**loses; losing; lost**) **1** no longer have something and be unable to find it: *I lost my keys.* **2** be beaten in a game or contest: *We lost by one goal.*

lottery noun (plural **lotteries**) a game in which you win money if the numbers on your ticket match the winning numbers.

loud adjective (**louder; loudest**) making a lot of noise: *The radio is too loud.*

love verb (**loves; loving; loved**) be very fond of someone or something.

lovely adjective (**lovelier; loveliest**) very pleasing to look at.

low adjective (**lower; lowest**) not measuring much from bottom to top; not high: *a low fence.*

lucky adjective (**luckier; luckiest**) having good luck.

luggage noun bags and suitcases that you take with you when you are traveling.

lump noun (plural **lumps**) **1** a piece of something: *a lump of clay.* **2** a small swelling on the body.

lunch noun (plural **lunches**) a meal that

you eat in the middle of the day.

luxury noun (plural **luxuries**) something expensive that you would like to have although you do not need it.

Mm

machine noun (plural **machines**) a piece of equipment with an engine that does a particular kind of work: *a washing machine.*

mad adjective (**madder; maddest**) **1** very angry: *She was really mad at me.* **2** insane: *It was a mad idea.*

magazine noun (plural **magazines**) a thin book with paper covers, containing different stories and pictures, which comes

out once a week or once a month.

magic noun in stories, the power that some characters have to make impossible things happen.

magician noun (plural **magicians**) **1** in stories, a character that has magic

powers. **2** an entertainer who performs tricks that appear to be done by magic.

magnet noun (plural **magnets**) a piece of metal that pulls pieces of iron and steel towards it.

magnificent adjective very good; wonderful: *a magnificent palace.*

magnifying glass noun (plural **magnifying glasses**) a piece of glass that

makes things look larger than they really are.

mail noun letters, cards, and packages that are sent out and delivered.

main adjective most important: *the main road.*

makeup noun things like lipstick, eye shadow, and mascara, which people use to make their faces look more attractive.

male adjective (of a person or animal) being a member of the sex that cannot have babies: *A male sheep is called a ram.*

mammal noun (plural **mammals**) a kind of animal in which the female gives birth to live babies and feeds them with milk from her body.

A B C D E F G H I J K L M N O P Q R S T U V W X Y Z

67

mango noun (plural **mangoes**) a fruit with a green and red skin and soft, sweet, juicy, yellow flesh.

manners noun a way of behaving and speaking: It's good manners to say "please" and "thank you."

map noun (plural **maps**) a drawing of a country or other place showing important features.

marble noun (plural **marbles**) 1 a very hard stone used for statues, pillars, floors, etc. 2 a very small ball made of colored glass, used in playing a game called marbles.

march verb (**marches; marching; marched**) walk like a soldier, with quick, regular steps.

margin noun (plural **margins**) a blank space down the side of a page with writing or printing on it.

mark noun (plural **marks**) 1 a stain on something: There is a pen mark on this shirt. 2 a written or printed symbol: A punctuation mark.

market noun (plural **markets**) a place, often outdoors, where people sell lots of different things from stalls.

marmalade noun a kind of jam made from oranges, lemons, or limes.

marry verb (**marries; marrying; married**) become someone's husband or wife: She married her first boyfriend.

mask noun (plural **masks**) something that you wear over your face as a disguise or for protection.

massive adjective extremely large: a massive crowd of 20,000 people.

mast noun (plural **masts**) a tall pole to which the sail of a boat is attached.

mat noun (plural **mats**) 1 a small rug. 2 something that you put under a glass, cup, or plate to protect the table underneath.

match noun (plural **matches**) 1 a small wooden stick that you strike against a rough surface to make a flame. 2 a game between two teams or two players: a soccer match.
+ verb (**matches; matching; matched**) 1 be the same as something else: Your answers match mine. 2 look good with something else: Does this bag match these shoes?

material noun (plural **materials**) 1 something that things are made from, for example wood or paper. 2 cloth.

mathematics noun a subject in which you learn about numbers, shapes, and measurement.

mattress noun (plural **mattresses**) the large, thick pad that you lie on in a bed.

maze noun (plural **mazes**) a place with paths that are laid out in such as way as to make it difficult to find your way, like a puzzle.

meal noun (plural **meals**) food that you eat at a particular time of day: Breakfast is the most important meal of the day.

mean verb (**means; meaning; meant**) 1 (of a word, etc.) describe or show something: "Jacket" means "a short coat." 2 do something deliberately: I didn't mean to upset you.
+ adjective (**meaner; meanest**) 1 not willing to spend money or give things to people: He is too mean to give to charity. 2 unpleasant or unkind: She has a mean temper.

meaning noun (plural **meanings**) what a word or phrase means.

measles noun a children's illness that gives you small, red, itchy spots on your body.

measure verb (**measures; measuring; measured**) check the size of something.

medal noun (plural **medals**) a piece of metal that is awarded to someone who has won something or done something brave.

medicine noun (plural **medicines**) something that you take when you are ill to make you feel better.

medium adjective being in the middle between two extremes: These T-shirts come in small, medium, and large.

melon noun (plural **melons**) a large fruit with thick skin and soft, sweet, juicy flesh.

melt verb (**melts; melting; melted**) (of a solid) become liquid as a result of becoming warmer: Eat your ice cream before it melts in the sun.

member noun (plural **members**) a person who belongs to a group: I am a member of the computer club.

memory noun (plural **memories**) 1 your ability to remember things: I have a good memory for names. 2 something that you remember: happy memories of a vacation to the beach. 3 in a computer, the part that stores information.

mend verb (**mends; mending; mended**) fix something that is broken.

menu noun (plural **menus**) 1 the list of foods and drinks that are available to order in a restaurant. 2 in a computer, a list of choices.

mermaid noun (plural **mermaids**) in stories, a creature with the top half of a woman and the bottom half of a fish.

mess noun (plural **messes**) an untidy state.

message noun (plural **messages**) a piece of information that you send to someone or leave for someone.

metal noun (plural **metals**) a hard, strong material such as iron or gold.

method noun (plural **methods**) a way of working.

microchip noun (plural **microchips**) one of the very small pieces in a computer that make it work.

microphone noun (plural **microphones**) a piece of equipment that you speak or sing into to record your voice or to make it louder.

microscope noun (plural **microscopes**) a piece of equipment that makes very small things look larger.

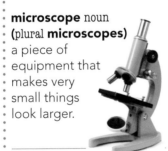

microwave noun (plural **microwaves**) a kind of oven in which you can cook food very quickly.

midday noun twelve o'clock in the middle of the day.

middle noun the part of something that is about halfway between the outer edges.

midnight noun twelve o'clock at night.

milk noun 1 the white liquid that female mammals produce to feed their babies. 2 the milk of a cow or a goat, which people can drink.

millionaire noun (plural **millionaires**) a person who has more than a million dollars.

mince noun beef or other meat that has been cut into tiny pieces.

mind noun (plural **minds**) your ability to think, along with all your thoughts and memories.
+ verb (**minds; minding; minded**) be upset or annoyed: I hope you don't mind that I ate the last piece of cake.

mine noun (plural **mines**) a hole dug very deep in the ground, where people dig out coal, gold, diamonds, etc.

mint noun (plural **mints**) 1 a green plant with strong-tasting leaves that are used in cooking. 2 a candy that tastes like mint.

minus preposition in mathematics, take away: 5 minus 3 is 2.
+ adjective in mathematics, being less than zero: The temperature fell to minus ten degrees.

minute noun (plural **minutes**) a period of 60 seconds.
+ adjective extremely small; tiny.

miracle noun (plural **miracles**) something wonderful that happens although it seemed impossible, which some people believe God has caused to happen.

mirror noun (plural **mirrors**) a special piece of glass that you can see yourself in.

mischievous adjective naughty in a playful way.

miserable adjective very unhappy.

miss verb (**misses; missing; missed**) 1 fail to catch or hit something: I threw a dart but it completely missed the dartboard. 2 be too late to catch a bus or train. 3 be sad because you are not with someone.

mist noun (plural **mists**) a thick cloud made up of tiny drops of water that hangs in the air and makes it difficult to see.

mistake noun (plural **mistakes**) something that you have done wrong: I made two mistakes on my test.

mix verb (**mixes; mixing; mixed**) put things together: Mix red and blue paint to make purple.

mixture noun (plural **mixtures**) something that is made of two or more things mixed together: a mixture of raspberries and strawberries.

moan verb (**moans; moaning; moaned**) make a low sound because you are in pain or unhappy.

mobile adjective that can be moved about: a mobile library.
+ noun (plural **mobiles**) **1** a decoration that dangles from the ceiling, moving about when there is a breeze. **2** a mobile phone.

mobile phone noun (plural **mobile phones**) a small telephone that you can easily carry around with you.

model noun (plural **models**) **1** a small copy of something: a model of a railway train. **2** a person who shows how clothes look by being photographed, or walking up and down, while wearing them.

modern adjective using new ideas; not old-fashioned: a modern kitchen.

modest adjective not boastful.

moisture noun dampness: There is a lot of moisture in the air.

mold noun **1** a green or gray substance that forms on food that is no longer fresh. **2** a container used to make a liquid set in a particular shape.

mole noun (plural **moles**) **1** a small animal with smooth, dark fur that digs tunnels in the ground. **2** a small dark spot on your skin.

moment noun (plural **moments**) a very short time: I'll be with you in a moment.

money noun coins and bills that you use to buy things.

mongrel noun (plural **mongrels**) a dog that has parents of different breeds.

monkey noun (plural **monkeys**) a furry wild animal with a long tail, which swings from tree to tree in the jungle.

monster noun (plural **monsters**) in stories, a large, frightening creature.

moon noun the large, round object that shines in the sky at night.

mop noun (plural **mops**) a tool for washing floors, consisting of a long handle with pieces of string attached to the end.

morning noun (plural **mornings**) the early part of the day, between night and afternoon.

mosque noun (plural **mosques**) a building

where Muslims go to worship.

mosquito noun (plural **mosquitoes**) a small flying insect that bites people and animals.

moss noun (plural **mosses**) a flat, green plant that grows on the ground, on trees, or on walls.

moth noun (plural **moths**) an insect with large wings, which looks like a butterfly but less colorful.

mother noun (plural **mothers**) a female parent.

motor noun (plural **motors**) an engine that makes a vehicle or machine work.

motorcycle noun (plural **motorcycles**) a vehicle with two wheels and an engine.

mountain noun (plural **mountains**) an area of very high land, higher than a hill.

mouse noun (plural **mice**) **1** a small, furry animal with a long tail. **2** a small object that you use to move things around on a computer screen.

mouth noun (plural **mouths**) **1** the part of your face below your nose, which you use for eating and speaking. **2** the widest part of a river, where it flows into the sea.

mud noun earth mixed with water.

muddle noun (plural **muddles**) an untidy state in which things are mixed up.

mug noun (plural **mugs**) a large cup: a mug of hot chocolate.

multiply verb (**multiplies; multiplying; multiplied**) in mathematics, make a number bigger by a certain number of times: 5 multiplied by 2 is 10.

mumps noun a children's illness that gives you a sore throat and a swollen face and neck.

muscle noun (plural **muscles**) one of the parts inside your body that makes it move.

museum noun (plural **museums**) a place where people can go to look at objects of interest and importance, often from the past.

mushroom noun a small plant with a thick stem and a round top, which you can eat.

music noun the sounds that people make when they sing or play musical instruments.

musician noun (plural **musicians**) a person who plays a musical instrument.

mustache noun (plural **mustaches**) hair that grows above a man's top lip.

mustard noun a spicy, yellow sauce eaten cold

and used to add flavor to food.

mutter verb (**mutters; muttering; muttered**) say something in a low voice.

mystery noun (plural **mysteries**) something that cannot be explained or understood.

nail noun (plural **nails**) 1 the thin, hard part at the end of each of your fingers and toes. 2 a small, pointed piece of metal, which you hammer into objects to fasten them together.

naked adjective wearing no clothes.

name noun (plural **names**) what a person or thing is called.

narrow adjective (**narrower; narrowest**) being a short distance from side to side; not wide: a narrow street.

nasty adjective (**nastier; nastiest**) unpleasant or unkind.

natural adjective 1 produced or caused by nature: an area of great natural beauty. 2 to be expected; normal: It's natural to be shy when you first meet people.

nature noun (plural **natures**) 1 everything in the world that was not created by human beings, such as animals, plants, rivers, and mountains. 2 the kind of person you are: She has a sweet nature.

naughty adjective (**naughtier; naughtiest**) (of a child) behaving badly.

navy noun (plural **navies**) an organized group of people who fight for their country at sea if there is a war.

neat adjective (**neater; neatest**) clean and tidy.

necessary adjective that has to be done: We have made the necessary changes.

neck noun (plural **necks**) the part of your body that joins your head to your shoulders.

necklace noun (plural **necklaces**) a piece of jewelry that you wear around your neck.

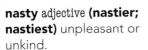

needle noun (plural **needles**) 1 a small, thin, pointed piece of metal used for sewing. 2 one of a pair of long, thin, pointed pieces of metal or plastic used for knitting. 3 one of the thin, pointed leaves of a pine tree.

neighbor noun (plural **neighbors**) a person who lives in the next house or in a house nearby.

nephew noun (plural **nephews**) the son of your brother or sister.

nerve noun (plural **nerves**) 1 one of the thin threads that carry messages between your brain and other parts of your body so that you can feel and move. 2 courage: I didn't have the nerve to complain.

nervous adjective slightly afraid and worried: I felt a bit nervous before the exam.

nest noun (plural **nests**) a home that a bird, mouse, or other small animal makes for its babies with twigs and leaves.

net noun (plural **nets**) 1 a piece of material made from threads or string with small spaces in between, sometimes used for fishing. 2 the Internet.

netball noun a game that is played between two teams who try to score goals by throwing a ball through a net at the top of a pole.

nettle noun (plural **nettles**) a wild plant with leaves that can sting you.

network noun (plural **networks**) a number of computers that are connected to each other.

new adjective (**newer; newest**) **1** that has just been produced or bought: a new film. **2** different: Nicole's new boyfriend.

news noun information about things that have just happened.

newspaper noun (plural **newspapers**) a number of large sheets of paper folded together and printed with news stories and photographs.

nibble verb (**nibbles; nibbling; nibbled**) eat something with small bites.

nice adjective (**nicer; nicest**) **1** (of a person) kind and friendly. **2** (of a thing) pleasant or enjoyable: Did you have a nice holiday?

nickname noun (plural **nicknames**) a name that a person's friends and family

sometimes call them: Robert's nickname is Bobby.

niece noun (plural **nieces**) the daughter of your brother or sister.

nightmare noun (plural **nightmares**) a frightening dream.

nod verb (**nods; nodding; nodded**) move your head up and down to show that you agree.

noise noun (plural **noises**) a sound, especially a loud one.

nonsense noun silly words that make no sense.

noon noun twelve o'clock in the middle of the day.

north noun one of the four main points of the compass, to the left when you are facing the direction where the sun rises.

nose noun (plural **noses**) the part that sticks out from the middle of your face that you use to breathe and to smell things.

nostril noun (plural **nostrils**) one of the two openings in your nose through which you breathe.

note noun (plural **notes**) **1** a short letter. **2** a single sound in music. **3** in the UK, the name for a piece of printed paper used as money: a ten-pound note.

notice verb (**notices; noticing; noticed**) see or become aware of something: I didn't notice the rain had stopped. **+** noun (plural **notices**) a sign or poster giving information.

novel noun (plural **novels**) a book that tells a made-up story.

nudge verb (**nudges; nudging; nudged**) knock or bump someone, usually with your elbow.

nuisance noun someone or something that is annoying or troublesome.

numb adjective (of a part of your body) having no feeling in it: My fingers were numb with the cold.

number noun (plural **numbers**) a word or figure that tells you how many of something there are: The

number of people in our class is thirty.

numerous adjective very many.

nurse noun (plural **nurses**) a person who takes care of sick people in a hospital.

nursery noun (plural **nurseries**) a place where young children can be looked after during the day while their parents are working.

nut noun (plural **nuts**) a hard fruit that grows on certain trees, such as the walnut and almond.

Oo

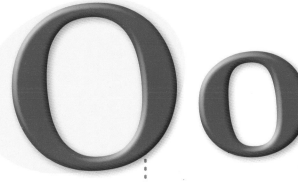

oak noun (plural **oaks**) a large tree with nuts called acorns.

oar noun (plural **oars**) a wooden pole with a flat part at one end, which is used for rowing a boat.

oasis noun (plural **oases**) a place in a desert where there is water and where trees grow.

oats noun a plant that is grown for its seeds, which are called grain and which are used for food for humans and animals.

obedient adjective doing what you are told to do.

obey verb (**obeys; obeying; obeyed**) do what someone tells you to do.

object noun (plural **objects**) anything that you can see and touch. + verb (**objects; objecting; objected**) dislike something or find it annoying: They object to people wearing shoes in the house.

oblong adjective a shape that is different from a square, circle, or sphere by being longer in one direction than another.

obstacle noun (plural **obstacles**) something that blocks your way.

obvious adjective very easy to see or understand.

occasion noun (plural **occasions**) **1** a time when something happens: on more than one occasion. **2** an important event: a new dress for a special occasion.

occupied adjective **1** (of a person) busy doing something: Taking care of a large family keeps her fully occupied. **2** (of a room, seat, etc.) that is being used: The bathroom is occupied at the moment.

occur verb (**occurs; occurring; occurred**) **1** happen. **2** (of an idea or thought) come into your mind: It occurred to me that you might need help.

ocean noun (plural **oceans**) a very large sea.

octopus noun (plural **octopuses; octopi**) a sea creature that has eight arms called tentacles.

odd adjective (**odder; oddest**) **1** strange or unusual. **2** (of a number) that cannot be divided exactly by two: Five is an odd number. **3** not matching: odd socks.

odor noun (plural **odors**) a smell, especially an unpleasant one.

offend verb (**offends; offending; offended**) upset or insult someone.

offer verb (**offers; offering; offered**) **1** ask someone if they would like something: She offered me a drink. **2** say you are willing to do something: I offered to do the dishes.

office noun (plural **offices**) a room where people work at desks.

officer noun (plural **officers**) **1** a person in the army, navy, or air force who gives orders to others. **2** a member of the police force.

official adjective done or organized by someone who is in charge: an official letter.

oil noun **1** a thick liquid that is taken out of the ground and used as a fuel, etc. **2** a thick liquid that is gotten from plants or animals and used in cooking: olive oil.

ointment noun (plural **ointments**) a kind of cream that you put on a cut or sore skin to make it better.

old adjective (**older; oldest**) **1** (of a person) having lived for a long time. **2** (of a thing) having been used for a long time: an old coat.

olive noun (plural **olives**) a small green or black fruit that can be eaten or used to make olive oil.

onion noun (plural **onions**) a small, round vegetable with a strong taste and a thin brown or purple skin.

open adjective not closed: an open window.
+ verb (**opens**; **opening**; **opened**) **1** move a door or window so that it is no longer closed. **2** take the lid off something: I opened a bottle of milk.

opera noun (plural **operas**) a kind of play in which all the words are sung rather than spoken.

operation noun (plural **operations**) the cutting open of a patient's body by a doctor to remove or fix a damaged part.

opinion noun (plural **opinions**) what you think about a particular subject: In my opinion, cats make the best pets.

opponent noun (plural **opponents**) a person who is on the other side from you in an argument or a game.

opportunity noun (plural **opportunities**) a chance to do something: He got the opportunity to go to Japan.

opposite preposition facing: the house opposite ours.

+ noun (plural **opposites**) something that is as different from something else as it is possible to be: Heat is the opposite of cold.

optometrist noun (plural **optometrists**) a person who tests people's eyesight and prescribes glasses and contact lenses.

orange noun (plural **oranges**) a round, juicy fruit with thick, orange-colored skin.
+ adjective of the color of an orange; reddish-yellow.

orchard noun (plural **orchards**) a place where fruit trees are grown.

orchestra noun (plural **orchestras**) a large group of people who play musical instruments together.

order noun (plural **orders**) **1** an instruction or command: The soldiers were just following orders. **2** the way something is organized: in alphabetical order.
+ verb (**orders**; **ordering**; **ordered**) **1** tell someone to do something. **2** ask for food or a drink in a restaurant: I ordered a hamburger.

ordinary adjective not special or unusual: just an ordinary guy.

organ noun (plural **organs**) **1** a large musical instrument with a keyboard, similar to a piano but with large air pipes where the sound comes out. **2** a part of your body, such as your heart or stomach, that does an important job.

organize verb (**organizes**; **organizing**; **organized**) arrange or plan something: We are organizing a trip to the beach.

original adjective **1** being the first version of something, rather than a copy: This is an original painting by this artist, not a print. **2** (of an idea) new and not copied from someone else's ideas.

ornament noun (plural **ornaments**) an object that has no practical use but is nice to look at.

orphan noun (plural **orphans**) a child whose parents are both dead.

ostrich noun (plural **ostriches**) a very large bird that cannot fly but can run fast.

outline noun (plural **outlines**) the shape of something, as if there was a line drawn around it.

oval noun (plural **ovals**) a shape that looks like an egg.

oven noun (plural **ovens**) a heated chamber where you can bake or roast food.

owe verb (**owes**; **owing**; **owed**) have to pay back money that you have borrowed from someone: I owe you ten dollars.

owl noun (plural **owls**) a bird with big eyes that is active at night.

own
verb (**owns**; **owning**; **owned**) have or possess something.
+ adjective belonging to someone: Adam brought his own sleeping bag.

owner noun (plural **owners**) the person that something belongs to.

ox noun (plural **oxen**) a bull that is used for pulling carts or carrying things.

oyster noun (plural **oysters**) a large, flat shellfish that produces pearls.

Pp

paddle verb (**paddles; paddling; paddled**)
1 walk in shallow water.
2 make a small boat move through water by using a special oar called a paddle.

page noun (plural **pages**) one side of a sheet of paper in a book, newspaper, or magazine.

pain noun (plural pains) the unpleasant feeling you have when a part of your body hurts.

paint noun (plural **paints**) a colored liquid that you use to make a picture or to cover a wall, ceiling, etc.
+ verb (**paints; painting; painted**) use paint to make a picture or cover a

wall, etc.: I have painted my bedroom purple.

painting noun (plural **paintings**) a picture of something that has been made using paint.

palace noun (plural **palaces**) a very grand building that is the home of a king, queen, or some presidents.

pale adjective (**paler; palest**) not dark or bright in color: a pale blue shirt.

palm noun (plural **palms**) **1** the flat part on the inside of your hand. **2** a tree that

grows in hot places, with long leaves growing out of the top of a tall trunk.

pancake noun (plural **pancakes**) a thin, flat, fried cake made of flour, milk and eggs.

panda noun (plural **pandas**) a large bearlike animal with black and white fur.

panic verb (**panics; panicking; panicked**) have a sudden, strong feeling of worry or fear.

panther noun (plural **panthers**) a large wild animal of the cat family with black fur.

paper noun (plural **papers**)
1 a material made from wood, which you write on.
2 a newspaper.

parachute noun (plural **parachutes**) a large piece of cloth with strings attached, by which a person can float safely to the ground from an airplane.

parade noun (plural **parades**) a large number of people marching along a road, often because it is a special occasion.

parent noun (plural **parents**) your mother or father.

park noun (plural **parks**) an area of land with grass and trees, where people can walk or play.
+ verb (**parks; parking; parked**) leave your car for a while in the street or in a garage or lot.

parrot noun (plural **parrots**) a large, brightly colored bird that people sometimes keep as a pet.

partner noun (plural **partners**) a person that you are paired with for dancing, playing a game, etc.

party noun (plural **parties**) a group of people invited to have fun together, often because it is a special occasion such as a birthday.

pass verb (**passes; passing; passed**) **1** walk past someone or something. **2** hand something to someone: *Would you please pass the ketchup?* **3** do well in an exam or test.

passage noun (plural **passages**) a space or path which something or someone can go through.

passenger noun (plural **passengers**) a person, other than the driver, who is traveling in a vehicle.

passport noun (plural **passports**) a book with your photograph and personal details in it, which you need to take with you when you travel to another country.

pasta noun a kind of food made from flour and water, which is formed into different shapes: spaghetti, lasagna, and other kinds of pasta.

pastime noun (plural **pastimes**) something that you do because you enjoy it or are interested in it.

pastry noun a mixture of flour, fat, and water that is used to make pies and other sweet baked goods.

patient noun (plural **patients**) a person who is being treated by a doctor. **+ adjective** able to wait calmly without getting annoyed.

pattern noun (plural **patterns**) a regular arrangement of lines and shapes.

pause verb (**pauses; pausing; paused**) stop for a short time while you are talking or doing something. **+ noun** (plural **pauses**) a short time when you stop while you are talking or doing something.

pavement noun (plural **pavements**) a hard surface made of concrete or asphalt.

paw noun (plural **paws**) an animal's foot.

pay verb (**pays; paying; paid**) give someone money in exchange for something that you are buying.

pea noun (plural **peas**) a small, round, green vegetable that grows inside a pod.

peace noun **1** a time of no war. **2** a calm, quiet state.

peach noun (plural **peaches**) a round fruit with a fuzzy, yellow and red skin and soft, juicy, yellow flesh.

a b c d e f g h i j k l m n o p q r s t u v w x y z

peacock noun (plural **peacocks**) a large bird with bright blue and green feathers and a long tail that it can spread out like a fan.

peanut noun (plural **peanuts**) a small, round nut that grows in a pod under the ground.

pear noun (plural **pears**) a juicy fruit narrow at the top and rounded at the bottom.

pebble noun (plural **pebbles**) a small, smooth, round stone.

peculiar adjective strange or odd.

pearl noun (plural **pearls**) a small, round, shiny, whitish object that grows inside an oyster's shell and which is used to make jewelry.

pedal noun (plural **pedals**) a part of a bicycle, car, etc., that you operate by pressing with your foot.

pedestrian noun (plural **pedestrians**) a person who is walking rather than driving.

peek verb (**peeks; peeking; peeked**) look quickly at someone or something.

peel verb (**peels; peeling; peeled**) remove the skin from a fruit or vegetable.

pelican noun (plural **pelicans**) a large white water bird with a large beak that it can store fish in before eating them.

penguin noun (plural **penguins**) a large black and white bird that cannot fly and which lives in the Antarctic.

pepper noun (plural **peppers**) **1** a hot-tasting powder used to add flavor to food. **2** a red, green, yellow, or orange vegetable, which can be eaten raw or cooked.

percussion adjective (of a musical instrument) that you play by striking it: I play a drum in the percussion band.

perfect adjective that could not be better; having no faults: a perfect score of 10 out of 10.

perform verb (**performs; performing; performed**) do something to entertain people, such as singing, dancing or acting.

perfume noun a liquid that you put on your skin to smell nice.

period noun (plural **periods**) a length of time: a period of two weeks.

permanent adjective lasting forever or for a long time.

permit verb (**permits; permitting; permitted**) allow someone to do something.

persuade verb (**persuades; persuading; persuaded**) convince someone that they should do something by giving good reasons why they should.

pet noun (plural **pets**) an animal, such as a cat or dog, that you look after and keep in your home.

photocopy noun (plural **photocopies**) an exact copy of a document that is made using a machine called a photocopier.

photograph noun (plural **photographs**) a picture of someone or something that is made using a camera.

picnic noun (plural **picnics**) a light meal that you take with you to eat outside.

picture noun (plural **pictures**) a painting, drawing, or photograph.

pig noun (plural **pigs**) an animal with a curly tail that is kept on a farm for its meat.

pigeon noun (plural **pigeons**) a large grey bird, which often lives in a city.

piano noun (plural **pianos**) a large musical instrument that you play by pressing the black and white keys on its keyboard.

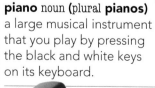

petal noun (plural **petals**) one of the white or colored parts of a flower.

phone noun (plural **phones**) a telephone. + verb (**phones; phoning; phoned**) call someone on the telephone.

pie noun (plural **pies**) a pastry case with meat or fruit inside.

pill noun (plural **pills**) a small ball of medicine, which you swallow.

pillow noun (plural **pillows**) a soft pad that you lay your head on in bed.

pilot noun (plural **pilots**) a person who flies an airplane.

pine noun (plural **pines**) a tall tree with thin, pointed leaves called needles, which do not fall off in autumn.

pink adjective (**pinker; pinkest**) pale red.

pirate noun (plural **pirates**) a person who attacks and steals from ships.

pit noun (plural **pits**) **1** a very deep hole in the ground. **2** a small hole or dent on a surface.

pitch noun (plural **pitches**) **1** how high or low a sound is. **2** the throw of a baseball or softball to a batter.

pity noun a feeling of sorrow for someone who is unhappy or unfortunate. **+ verb** (**pities; pitying; pitied**) feel sorry for someone who is unhappy or unfortunate.

pineapple noun (plural **pineapples**) a large fruit with thick, bumpy skin and sweet, juicy, yellow flesh.

pizza noun (plural **pizzas**) a flat circle of dough topped with tomatoes, cheese, herbs, and sometimes other vegetables or meat.

plane noun (plural **planes**) an airplane.

planet noun (plural **planets**) a very large object in space that moves around the sun.

plaster noun (plural **plasters**) **1** a small strip of material that you use to cover a cut in your skin to keep it clean. **2** a kind of powder mixed with water, which dries hard and is used to smooth over walls and ceilings.

plastic noun a light, strong, manufactured material that can be used to make many different things: plastic cups.

plate noun (plural **plates**) a round, flat dish that you eat from.

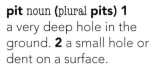

platform noun (plural **platforms**) **1** the part of a station where you wait for a train to arrive. **2** a raised area in a room or hall that people can stand on.

play verb (**plays; playing; played**) **1** have fun, usually by taking part in a game. **2** make music with a musical instrument: Can you play the guitar? **+ noun** (plural **plays**) a story that people act out on a stage, or on television or radio.

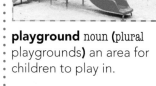

playground noun (plural **playgrounds**) an area for children to play in.

pleasant adjective nice, pleasing or enjoyable: a pleasant afternoon at the bowling alley.

please verb (**pleases; pleasing; pleased**) make someone happy.

A B C D E F G H I J K L M N O **P** Q R S T U V W X Y Z

pleasure noun a feeling of enjoyment or happiness.

pleat noun (plural **pleats**) a folded part of a skirt, dress, etc. that has been pressed or stitched in place.

plot noun (plural **plots**) **1** a secret plan. **2** the story of a book or film.

plug noun (plural **plugs**) **1** a piece of rubber that you put in the drain hole in a sink or bath to stop the water from draining. **2** the part of a piece of electrical equipment that you put into an electrical socket to make it work.

plum noun (plural **plums**) a small fruit with smooth, thin skin and soft, sweet, juicy flesh.

plumber noun (plural **plumbers**) a person who fits and repairs water pipes.

plump adjective (**plumper; plumpest**) slightly fat.

plus preposition in mathematics, added to: 5 plus 3 is 8.

pocket noun (plural **pockets**) a small pouch sewn into a piece of clothing that you can keep things in.

poem noun (plural **poems**) a piece of writing in short lines that has a rhythm and often rhymes.

poet noun (plural **poets**) a person who writes poems.

point noun (plural **points**) **1** the sharp end of something such as a pin or needle. **2** a time or position: At that point in the movie, everyone laughed. **3** the reason for doing something: The whole point of going into town was to buy a DVD. **4** a mark that you score in a game or contest. + verb (**points; pointing; pointed**) stick out your finger in the direction of someone or something.

poison noun (plural **poisons**) a substance that can make you very ill or kill you if you swallow it.

poke verb (**pokes; poking; poked**) push someone or something with your finger or with a pointed object.

polar bear noun (plural **polar bears**) a very large white bear that lives in the Arctic.

pole noun (plural **poles**) a long, rounded piece of metal, plastic, or wood.

police noun a group of people whose job is to make sure that people do not break the law and to arrest people if they do break the law.

polish noun (plural **polishes**) a substance that you use to make something shiny. + verb (**polishes; polishing; polished**) make something shiny by putting polish on it and rubbing it with a cloth.

polite adjective (**politer; politest**) having good manners; not rude.

pollen noun a yellow powder inside flowers, which is carried to other flowers by the wind or by insects to make seeds.

pond noun (plural **ponds**) a small area of fresh water.

pony noun (plural **ponies**) a small horse.

ponytail noun (plural **ponytails**) a hairstyle in which long hair is tied at the back of the head with the ends hanging down.

a b c d e f g h i j k l m n o p q r s t u v w x y z

pool noun (plural **pools**) a small area of water, especially one for swimming in.

poor adjective (**poorer**; **poorest**) **1** having very little money. **2** of bad quality; not good: That was a poor attempt. **3** unfortunate: Poor Stephen has broken his leg.

popcorn noun a snack made from grains of corn that have been heated till they burst open and puff up.

poppy noun (plural **poppies**) a large, red wildflower.

popular adjective liked by many people.

population noun (plural **populations**) the number of people living in a particular place.

porch noun (plural **porches**) a sheltered area at the entrance to a building.

porcupine noun (plural **porcupines**) a large animal that is covered in spines.

pork noun meat that comes from a pig.

port noun (plural **ports**) a place on the coast where boats load and unload.

portable adjective that can be easily carried about: a portable television.

portion noun (plural **portions**) the amount of food that is given to one person.

portrait noun (plural **portraits**) a picture of a person.

possess verb (**possesses**; **possessing**; **possessed**) own something.

possible adjective **1** that can be done. **2** that might happen: It's possible that it will snow tomorrow.

post noun (plural **posts**) **1** a wooden or metal pole that is fixed in the ground. **2** something published online: I published my blog post.
+ verb (**posts**; **posting**; **posted**) send a letter, card, or package to someone.

postcard noun (plural **postcards**) a thin piece of card, often with a picture on one side, on which you can write a message

on and then mail it to someone.

poster noun (plural **posters**) a large picture or notice that you put on a wall.

postman noun (plural **postmen**) a person who delivers letters, cards, and packages to people's homes.

post office noun (plural **post offices**) a building where you can take letters, cards, and packages to be mailed.

postpone verb (**postpones**; **postponing**; **postponed**) change an appointment or arrangement to a later date.

potato noun (plural **potatoes**) a common round vegetable that grows under the ground.

pour verb (**pours; pouring; poured**) **1** tip a container so that the liquid inside flows out: I poured some tea into a cup. **2** rain heavily.

practice noun doing something repeatedly in order to become better at doing it: piano practice. **+ verb (practices; practicing; practiced)** do something repeatedly in order to become better at doing it.

prairie noun (plural **prairies**) a large area of mostly flat grassland.

praise verb (**praises; praising; praised**) tell someone that they have done something well.

prank noun (plural **pranks**) a trick played on someone.

precious adjective **1** worth a lot of money: precious jewels. **2** very special or dear to someone: her precious daughter.

precise adjective exact or accurate.

predict verb (**predicts; predicting; predicted**) say what is going to happen in the future.

prefer verb (**prefers; preferring; preferred**) like one person or thing better than another.

prepare verb (**prepares; preparing; prepared**) get something or yourself ready.

present noun (plural **presents**) **1** something you give to someone; a gift. **2** the time now: There's nobody home at present. **+ verb (presents; presenting; presented)** give something to someone as a gift or award. **+ adjective** that is here: The whole class was present.

president noun (plural **presidents**) the person who is in charge of a country or an organization.

pretend verb (**pretends; pretending; pretended**) say or act as if something untrue is true: He pretended to be a newspaper reporter.

pretty adjective (**prettier; prettiest**) very pleasing to look at.

prevent verb (**prevents; preventing; prevented**) stop something from happening.

price noun (plural **prices**) the amount of money that you pay to buy something.

pride noun a proud feeling.

prince noun (plural **princes**) the son of a king or queen.

princess noun (plural **princesses**) **1** the daughter of a king or queen. **3** the wife of a prince.

print verb (**prints; printing; printed**) **1** write words without joining the letters together. **2** make many copies of a book, newspaper, or magazine using a special machine.

powder noun (plural **powders**) a substance that has been ground into tiny pieces: powder foundation.

a b c d e f g h i j k l m n o p q r s t u v w x y z

printer noun (plural **printers**) **1** a machine connected to a computer that can print information from the computer onto paper. **2** a person who prints books, newspapers, or magazines.

print-out noun (plural **print-outs**) a printed copy of information from a computer.

prison noun (plural **prisons**) a place where criminals are locked up; a jail.

private adjective that is for one person or one group of people only.

prize noun (plural **prizes**) something that you get for winning a competition or game.

probable adjective likely to be the case: It's probable that our team will win the tournament.

problem noun (plural **problems**) something that is difficult to deal with or to understand.

profit noun (plural **profits**) the money that you make by selling something for more than it cost you to buy it or make it.

program noun (plural **programs**) **1** a show on television or radio. **2** a small book giving information about a concert, play or other event. **3** a set of instructions that a computer follows.

project noun (plural **projects**) a piece of work in which you gather information about a particular topic and then write about it or present it.

promise verb (**promises; promising; promised**) say that you definitely will do something: I promise I will clean my room.

proof noun (plural **proofs**) facts that show that something is definitely true.

proper adjective right or correct: the proper way to do something.

property noun (plural **properties**) the things that a person owns: This computer is Anil's property.

protect verb (**protects; protecting; protected**) look after someone or something to keep them safe.

protest verb (**protests; protesting; protested**) say that you disagree with something.

proud adjective (**prouder; proudest**) pleased with something that you have done or that you possess: He was very proud of the story he had written.

prove verb (**proves; proving; proved**) show that something is definitely true.

public adjective that is for anyone to use; not private: the public swimming pool.

pudding noun (plural **puddings**) a soft, creamy dessert.

puddle noun (plural **puddles**) a small pool of water that forms when it has been raining.

pulse noun (plural **pulses**) the regular beating of your blood as it is pumped around your body by your heart.

pump noun (plural **pumps**) a machine that forces air or water into or out of something: a bicycle pump. + verb (**pumps; pumping; pumped**) force air or water into or out of something by using a pump.

pumpkin noun (plural **pumpkins**) a large, round, orange vegetable with a thick skin.

punch verb (**punches; punching; punched**) hit someone with your fist.

puncture noun (plural **punctures**) a small hole in a tire, which causes the air to come out and the tire to become flat.

punish verb (**punishes; punishing; punished**) make someone suffer because of something that they have done wrong.

pupil noun (plural **pupils**) **1** a child in school. **2** the small, black circle in the middle of your eye.

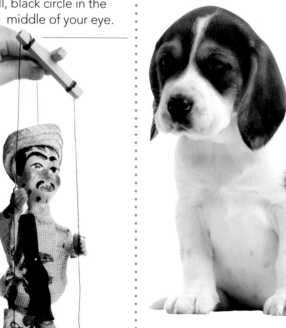

puppet noun (plural **puppets**) a kind of

doll that you can make move by pulling strings that are attached to it or by moving your hand inside it.

puppy noun (plural **puppies**) a young dog.

pure adjective (**purer; purest**) not mixed with anything: pure orange juice.

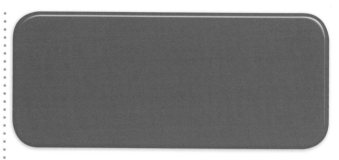

purple adjective of a reddish-blue color.

purpose noun (plural **purposes**) your reason for doing something; intention.

purr verb (**purrs; purring; purred**) (of a cat) make a low sound in its throat because it is happy.

purse noun (plural **purses**) **1** a small bag or pouch to keep your money in. **2** a handbag.

puzzle noun (plural **puzzles**) **1** a game in which you have to find the answers to a difficult problem. **2** something that is difficult to understand. verb (**puzzles; puzzling; puzzled**) make someone confused and unable to understand.

push verb (**pushes; pushing; pushed**) press something hard with your hands to move it away from you: He pushed the box out of the way.

put verb (**puts; putting; put**) place something somewhere: Put your toys in the toy box.

python noun (plural **pythons**) a snake that can crush animals to death by wrapping its body tightly around them.

Qq

qualify verb (**qualifies; qualifying; qualified**)
1 pass an exam that is needed to be able to do a job: David has qualified as a dentist. **2** in a competition, get enough points to get through to the next stage.

quality noun (plural **qualities**) a standard of how good or bad something is: paper of the highest quality.

quantity noun (plural **quantities**) an amount of something: a huge quantity of ice cream.

quarter noun (plural **quarters**) **1** one of four equal parts of something: The last quarter of the film was very exciting. **2** a US coin worth twenty-five cents.

queue noun (plural **queues**) a line of people waiting for something.

quick adjective (**quicker; quickest**) **1** moving or able to move fast: a quick runner. **2** lasting a very short time: a quick trip to the store.

quiet adjective (**quieter; quietest**) not making a lot of noise: a quiet voice.

quilt noun (plural **quilts**) a thick, light cover for a bed.

quiz noun (plural **quizzes**) a game in which one person asks questions and the other people try to answer them correctly.

quote verb (**quotes; quoting; quoted**) repeat what someone else has said, using exactly the same words.

quarrel verb (**quarrels; quarrelling; quarrelled**) argue with someone.

quarry noun (plural **quarries**) a place where people cut stone out of the land for building.

queen noun (plural **queens**) **1** a woman who rules a country. **2** the wife of a king.

query noun (plural **queries**) a question: I have a query about my phone bill.

question noun (plural **questions**) something that you ask when you want information.

Rr

rabbit noun (plural **rabbits**) a small, furry animal with long ears, which people sometimes keep as a pet.

radiator noun (plural **radiators**) a metal heater attached to a wall, which makes a room warm.

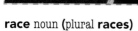

race noun (plural **races**) **1** a competition to see who is the fastest runner, swimmer, etc. **2** a large group of people who originally come from the same part of the world and look similar, for example in skin color and hair color.
+ verb (**races; racing; raced**) try to run or swim the fastest in a competition.

racket noun (plural **rackets**) **1** a kind of bat with crossed strings in the middle of a round frame, which is used to play tennis, badminton, or squash. **2** a loud noise: There was a terrible racket coming from the house next door.

radio noun (plural **radios**) a piece of equipment that receives signals through the air and which you can listen to programs on.

rag noun (plural **rags**) an old, torn piece of cloth.

rage noun extreme anger.

railway noun (plural **railways**) a system of metal rails that trains travel on.

rain noun water that falls in drops from the clouds.
+ verb (**rains; raining; rained**) fall in drops as rain from the clouds: It's raining heavily.

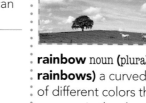

rainbow noun (plural **rainbows**) a curved band of different colors that appears in the sky when the sun shines through rain.

raisin noun (plural **raisins**) a dried grape.

rake noun (plural **rakes**) a garden tool with a long handle and a bar with teeth or prongs, which is used to turn over soil or gather leaves.

ram noun (plural **rams**) a male sheep.

rap verb (**raps; rapping; rapped**) knock or tap on a door.
+ noun (plural **raps**) a kind of music in which the words are spoken over a strong beat.

rapid adjective very fast: a rapid heartbeat.

rare adjective (**rarer; rarest**) that does not occur very often: a rare bird.

rash noun (plural **rashes**) a lot of red spots on your skin, sometimes caused by an illness such as chickenpox.

raspberry noun (plural **raspberries**) a small, soft, juicy, red fruit.

rat noun (plural **rats**) a small, furry animal with a very long tail, which looks like a large mouse.

rattle verb (**rattles; rattling; rattled**) make repeated short, rapid, knocking sounds. + noun (plural **rattles**) a baby's toy that rattles when it is shaken.

raw adjective (of food) not cooked.

ray noun (plural **rays**) a beam of sunlight.

razor noun (plural **razors**) a tool used for shaving.

read verb (**reads; reading; read**) look at and understand words that are written down.

rear noun (plural **rears**) the back part of something: There is a parking lot at the rear of the building.

reason noun (plural **reasons**) something that explains why something happened: The reason we're late is that the bus didn't turn up.

receive verb (**receives; receiving; received**) get something that someone gives or sends to you.

recent adjective that happened a short time ago: our recent trip to London.

recipe noun (plural **recipes**) instructions for cooking a dish.

recite verb (**recites; reciting; recited**) say

something, such as a poem, that you have learned, without reading it.

recorder noun (plural **recorders**) a musical instrument that you play by blowing into it and covering different holes to produce different notes.

recover verb (**recovers; recovering; recovered**) become well again after you have been ill.

rectangle noun (plural **rectangles**) a shape with two long sides of equal length and two shorter sides of equal length.

recycle verb (**recycles; recycling; recycled**) use something again, sometimes by turning trash into something else that can be used.

red adjective (**redder; reddest**) of the color of blood.

referee noun (plural **referees**) a person who makes sure the players follow the rules during a game.

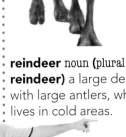

refreshments noun food and drinks served at an event such as a field day or a meeting.

refuse verb (**refuses; refusing; refused**) say that you will not do something: Kelly refused to help.

region noun (plural **regions**) a large area of a country.

regular adjective that always happens at the same time or on the same day: a regular trip to the swimming pool every Saturday.

rehearse verb (**rehearses; rehearsing; rehearsed**) practice for a performance: We are rehearsing for the school play.

reindeer noun (plural **reindeer**) a large deer with large antlers, which lives in cold areas.

relative noun (plural **relatives**) a member of your family.

relax verb (**relaxes; relaxing; relaxed**) stop worrying and become calm.

a
b
c
d
e
f
g
h
i
j
k
l
m
n
o
p
q
r
s
t
u
v
w
x
y
z

relay noun (plural **relays**) a kind of race in which teams take part, with each team member running or swimming for a part of the race.

relief noun a feeling of being glad that something bad or worrying is over.

religion noun (plural **religions**) a set of beliefs about God or gods and the ways that people worship them.

rely verb (**relies; relying; relied**) **1** need someone to help you: The old man relies on his daughter to cook his meals. **2** be able to trust someone: I am relying on you to do the right thing.

remain verb (**remains; remaining; remained**) stay in a place.

remark verb (**remarks; remarking; remarked**) say something about something; comment: "I like your new shoes," Sophie remarked.
+ noun (plural **remarks**) something that a person says about something; a comment: a rude remark.

remember verb (**remembers; remembering; remembered**) keep something in your mind; not forget.

remind verb (**reminds; reminding; reminded**) **1** help someone to remember something: Remind me to bring a change of clothes. **2** make someone think of another person because you are like them in some way: With your dark, curly hair you remind me of my brother.

remote adjective (**remoter; remotest**) (of a place) far away from towns and cities.

remote control noun (plural **remote controls**) an object that you hold in your hand, which has buttons you can press to switch a television, DVD player, etc., on and off from a distance.

repair verb (**repairs; repairing; repaired**) fix something that is broken.

repeat verb (**repeats; repeating; repeated**) say or do something again that you have said or done before.

reply verb (**replies; replying; replied**) answer someone.

report noun (plural **reports**) something written about a person or about a thing that has happened.

represent verb (**represents; representing; represented**) **1** (of a person) that has been chosen to speak for a group of people. **2** stand for or mean something: Fifty stars on the flag represent the fifty states of the USA.

reptile noun (plural **reptiles**) a kind of animal, such as a snake or a lizard, that has scales on its body and lays eggs.

rescue verb (**rescues; rescuing; rescued**) save someone from danger.

respect verb (**respects; respecting; respected**) have a very high opinion of someone and treat them politely.
+ noun admiration for someone.

responsible adjective **1** having caused a situation: Who is responsible for making this mess? **2** being in charge of a person or a situation: The teacher is responsible for the whole class. **3** sensible and trustworthy: a responsible adult.

rest noun (plural **rests**) **1** a time of lying down or relaxing. **2** the other people or things: David and the rest of the boys.
+ verb (**rests; resting; rested**) lie down or relax for a while.

restaurant noun (plural **restaurants**) a place where people can go to buy and eat a meal.

result noun (plural **results**) **1** something that happens because of something else: He lost a tooth as a result of a skateboarding accident. **2** the final score of a game or match: The result was a draw.

return verb (**returns; returning; returned**) **1** go back to a place. **2** give something back to someone: If you borrow a book from someone, remember to return it after you have read it.

reverse verb (**reverses; reversing; reversed**) to move in the opposite direction.

revise verb (**revises; revising; revised**) make changes that correct or improve something: I revised my essay.

reward noun (plural **rewards**) something that you are given for something good that you have done: If you work really hard at school, you will get a new bike as a reward.

ride verb (**rides; riding; rode; ridden**) **1** sit on a horse or a bicycle and guide it. **2** sit in a motor vehicle while it moves along.
+ noun (plural **rides**) a journey in a motor vehicle.

rinse verb (**rinses; rinsing; rinsed**) wash something in clear water to get rid of soap after washing it with soap.

rip verb (**rips; ripping; ripped**) tear something.

ripe adjective (**riper; ripest**) (of a fruit or vegetable) ready to eat.

robin noun (plural **robins**) a small, brown bird with a red chest.

rhinoceros noun (plural **rhinoceroses**) a very large wild animal with a thick skin and one or two horns on its nose.

rhyme verb (**rhymes; rhyming; rhymed**) (of two words) have a similar sound: "Cat" rhymes with "bat."

rhythm noun (plural **rhythms**) the regular beat in a piece of music.

ridiculous adjective does not make sense; silly or foolish: That's a ridiculous suggestion.

right adjective **1** correct or accurate: the right answer. **2** good or honest: Telling the truth was the right thing to do. **3** of the side that is opposite to left: I wear my watch on my right wrist.

river noun (plural **rivers**) a large stream of fresh water that flows into the sea.

robot noun (plural **robots**) a kind of machine that has been programmed to perform certain tasks that a human being could do.

rice noun small white or brown grains from a grass-like plant, which can be cooked and eaten.

rich adjective (**richer; richest**) having a lot of money.

ring noun (plural **rings**) a piece of jewelry in the shape of a circle, which you wear on your finger.
+ verb (**rings; ringing; rang; rung**) (of a bell) make a loud, high-pitched sound.

road noun (plural **roads**) a way from one place to another, with a hard surface for driving on.

roast verb (**roasts; roasting; roasted**) cook meat or vegetables in the oven.

rob verb (**robs; robbing; robbed**) steal things from someone.

rock noun (plural **rocks**) **1** a very large stone. **2** a hard, stony substance that is part of the earth's surface.
+ verb (**rocks; rocking; rocked**) move backward and forward or from side to side.

rocket noun (plural **rockets**) **1** a space vehicle shaped like a tube. **2** a kind of firework on a long stick, which shoots up high into the air.

rodent noun (plural **rodents**) a kind of animal, such as a mouse or squirrel, that has large, sharp front teeth.

roll verb (**rolls; rolling; rolled**) move along, turning over and over. + noun (plural **rolls**) **1** a long piece of paper or cloth that has been rolled into a tube shape. **2** a small loaf of bread for one person.

roof noun (plural **roofs**) the top outer surface of a building or vehicle.

room noun (plural **rooms**) **1** one of the parts that a building is divided into, separated from the other parts by walls. **2** the amount of space that something would take up: There is room for two cars in the garage.

root noun (plural **roots**) the part of a plant that grows under the ground.

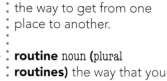

rope noun (plural **ropes**) a long piece of thick, strong twisted string.

rose noun (plural **roses**) a sweet-smelling flower with thorns on its stem.

rough adjective (**rougher; roughest**) **1** (of a surface) uneven; not smooth. **2** not gentle or careful: rough handling. **3** not exact: a rough guess.

round adjective (**rounder; roundest**) shaped like a circle.

route noun (plural **routes**) the way to get from one place to another.

routine noun (plural **routines**) the way that you usually do things.

row noun (plural **rows**) **1** a straight line of people or things. **2** a noisy argument. + verb (**rows; rowing; rowed**) make a small boat move through water by using oars.

royal adjective belonging to a king or queen: a royal palace.

rubber noun (plural **rubbers**) a material that stretches and bounces, used to make tires, balls, etc.

rubbish noun **1** things that have been thrown away because they are no longer wanted. **2** something that is of poor quality: That film was rubbish.

roller skate noun (plural **roller skates**) one of a pair of boots with small wheels attached to the bottom.

rude adjective (**ruder; rudest**) showing no respect; not polite.

rug noun (plural **rugs**) a carpet that covers a section of the floor.

rugby noun a game that is played between two teams who try to score goals by carrying an oval ball across a line or kicking it over a bar.

ruin verb (**ruins; ruining; ruined**) spoil or destroy something.
+ noun (plural **ruins**) a very old building that has partly crumbled away.

rule noun (plural **rules**) something that tells people what they must do and must not do
+ verb (**rules; ruling; ruled**) be in charge of a country.

ruler noun (plural **rulers**) **1** a person who rules a country. **2** a long, straight piece of plastic or wood that is used for measuring things or for drawing straight lines.

rumor noun (plural **rumors**) a story that people are talking about, which may or may not be true.

rush verb (**rushes; rushing; rushed**) move very quickly; hurry.

rust noun a rough, reddish-brown substance that forms on iron or steel that has gotten wet.

S s

saddle noun (plural **saddles**) a special kind of seat on a bicycle or for riding a horse.

salt noun a white powder that is used to flavor food.

sack noun (plural **sacks**) a large bag made of strong material.

sad adjective (**sadder; saddest**) **1** feeling unhappy. **2** causing someone to feel unhappy: a sad story.

safe adjective (**safer; safest**) **1** (of a person) in no danger. **2** (of a place) in which someone or something will be out of danger.
+ noun (plural **safes**) a strong metal box with a lock, where people keep money or valuable things.

sailor noun (plural **sailors**) a person who works on a ship.

salad noun (plural **salads**) a mixture of vegetables that are eaten raw, such as lettuce, cucumber, tomatoes, and peppers.

salmon noun (plural **salmon**) a large, silvery fish that people can eat.

sand noun very small grains of crushed rock, found on a beach or in a desert.

sandal noun (plural **sandals**) a kind of light shoe with straps, which you wear in warm weather.

sandwich noun (plural **sandwiches**) two pieces of bread with a filling in between: a cheese sandwich.

sari noun (plural **saris**) a long piece of cloth that is draped around the body and over one shoulder, worn mainly by South Asian women.

satisfy verb (**satisfies**; **satisfying**; **satisfied**) please someone by giving them what they want or need.

sauce noun (plural **sauces**) a thick liquid served with other food to add flavor: pasta with tomato sauce.

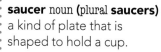

saucer noun (plural **saucers**) a kind of plate that is shaped to hold a cup.

sausage noun (plural **sausages**) a mixture of minced meat and spices put into a skin.

save verb (**saves**; **saving**; **saved**) **1** take someone out of a dangerous situation. **2** keep something, especially money, to use later.

saw noun (plural **saws**) a tool with sharp teeth along one edge, which is used for cutting wood. + verb (**saws**; **sawing**; **sawed**; **sawn**) cut something using a saw.

scales noun a device for weighing yourself or for weighing food, etc.

scar noun (plural **scars**) a mark that is sometimes left on your skin if it has been cut or burned and has then healed.

scarce adjective (**scarcer**; **scarcest**) not occurring frequently; rare.

scare verb (**scares**; **scaring**; **scared**) frighten someone.

scarecrow noun (plural **scarecrows**) a figure in the form of a man, made from sticks and old clothes, which is placed in a field of crops to frighten birds away.

scarf noun (plural **scarves**) a piece of soft material that you wear around your neck to keep it warm.

scheme noun (plural **schemes**) a clever or secret plan.

school noun (plural **schools**) a place where children are taught.

science noun (plural **sciences**) a subject in which you learn about things in the physical world around us.

scissors noun a tool with two sharp blades, which is used for cutting paper, cloth, or hair.

score noun (plural **scores**) in a game or contest, the number of points or goals that each contestant or team has made. + verb (**scores**; **scoring**; **scored**) in a game or contest, get a point or goal.

scream verb (**screams**; **screaming**; **screamed**) cry out in a loud, high-pitched voice because you are afraid or shocked.

sculpture noun (plural **sculptures**) a statue made out of stone, wood, metal, etc.

sea noun (plural **seas**) the salty water that covers a large part of the world's surface.

seal noun (plural **seals**) a large animal with flippers that lives mostly in the sea in cold areas.
✦ verb (**seals; sealing; sealed**) close an envelope by sticking down the flap.

season noun (plural **seasons**) one of the four parts that a year is divided into: spring, summer, autumn, and winter.

seat belt noun (plural **seat belts**) a strap that you fasten across your chest to keep you safe in a car.

seaweed noun a plant that grows in the sea.

second noun (plural **seconds**) a sixtieth part of a minute.

secret noun (plural **secrets**) something that very few people know and that they must not tell other people.

see verb (**sees; seeing; saw; seen**) **1** notice someone or something with your eyes. **2** understand something: I see what you mean.

seed noun (plural **seeds**) the small, hard part that a new plant grows from.

seesaw noun (plural **seesaws**) a kind of toy for two children to play on by sitting at either end of a long board and making it go up at one end and then the other.

select verb (**selects; selecting; selected**) choose or pick someone or something.

selfish adjective thinking only about yourself; not considering other people.

sell verb (**sells; selling; sold**) give something to someone in exchange for money.

sensible adjective knowing the right thing to do; wise.

sentence noun (plural **sentences**) a group of words that together mean something: The first sentence in the book is "I am an invisible man."

separate adjective not joined together.
✦ verb (**separates; separating; separated**) move people or things apart.

series noun (plural **series**) **1** a number of things one after the other: a series of accidents. **2** a television program that is shown in several parts: a six-part comedy series.

serious adjective **1** not smiling, laughing, or joking: The doctor looked very serious. **2** important: a serious matter. **3** very bad or dangerous: a serious illness.

servant noun (plural **servants**) a person who works in another person's house, looking after them and the house.

severe adjective (**severer; severest**) very bad; serious: a severe pain.

sew verb (**sews; sewing; sewed; sewn**) join pieces of cloth together using a needle and thread.

shade noun (plural **shades**) **1** a place that is sheltered from the sun: Keep the baby in the shade. **2** a degree of lightness or darkness of a color: a darker shade of green.

shadow noun (plural **shadows**) a dark shape caused by something blocking out the light.

shake verb (**shakes; shaking; shook; shaken**) **1** move something around quickly: She shook her hair out. **2** tremble because you are afraid or nervous.

shallow adjective (**shallower; shallowest**) does not go a long way down; not deep: a shallow puddle.

shampoo noun (plural **shampoos**) a soapy liquid for washing your hair with.

shape noun (plural **shapes**) the outline of something: The bread was cut in the shape of a heart.

share verb (**shares; sharing; shared**) **1** split something so that each person can have a part of it: Share your chocolate bar with your brother. **2** (of two or more people) use something together: The two girls shared a room.

sheep noun (plural **sheep**) an animal that is kept on a farm for its meat and wool.

sheet noun (plural **sheets**) **1** a large piece of thin material that you put on a bed. **2** a thin, flat piece of paper, glass, etc.

shelter noun (plural **shelters**) a place that provides protection from danger or from the weather. ✦ verb (**shelters; sheltering; sheltered**) stay in a place for protection from danger or from the weather: We sheltered from the rain under the trees.

shine verb (**shines; shining; shone**) give out light; be bright.

shiver verb (**shivers; shivering; shivered**) tremble because you are cold or afraid.

shock noun (plural **shocks**) something that surprises and upsets you. ✦ verb (**shocks; shocking; shocked**) surprise and upset someone.

shoe noun (plural **shoes**) one of two matching things that you wear on your feet when you go outside.

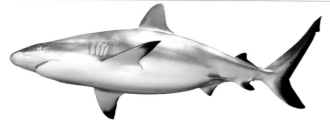

shark noun (plural **sharks**) a very large fish with rows of sharp teeth.

sharp adjective (**sharper; sharpest**) **1** having a fine cutting edge or point: a sharp knife. **2** sudden: a sharp pain.

ship noun (plural **ships**) a large boat.

shave verb (**shaves; shaving; shaved**) remove hair from your face, legs, etc., using a razor.

shed noun (plural **sheds**) a small building, often made of wood. ✦ verb (**sheds; shedding; shed**) (of a tree) lose its leaves in autumn.

shelf noun (plural **shelves**) a flat piece of wood or other material, attached to a wall or in a cupboard, that you can lay things on.

shell noun (plural **shells**) a hard, protective covering on a nut, egg, or some creatures such as a tortoise.

shirt noun (plural **shirts**) a piece of clothing, usually with sleeves and often with a collar, which you wear on the top part of your body.

shop noun (plural **shops**) a place where people go to buy things. ✦ verb (**shops; shopping; shopped**) go to stores to buy things.

short adjective (**shorter; shortest**) **1** not measuring much in length: a short skirt. **2** not lasting or taking up a lot of time: a short visit.

shorts noun short pants.

shoulder noun (plural **shoulders**) one of two parts of your body that start at the bottom of your neck and end at the top of your arms.

shout verb (**shouts; shouting; shouted**) say something in a loud voice.

shovel noun (plural **shovels**) a tool like a spade with a long handle and a curved metal part for scooping up earth, snow, etc.

shower noun (plural **showers**) **1** a short fall of rain or snow. **2** a kind of bath in which you stand up and water sprays down onto you.

shrink verb (**shrinks; shrinking; shrank; shrunk**) become smaller: My new sweater shrank in the wash.

shrug verb (**shrugs; shrugging; shrugged**) raise and lower your shoulders quickly to show that you do not know something or that you are not interested.

shut verb (**shuts; shutting; shut**) move something so that it covers an opening; close something: Shut the door!
+ adjective closed.

shy adjective (**shyer; shyest**) nervous and timid in company, especially with people you do not know well.

sick adjective (**sicker; sickest**) unwell.

sieve noun (plural **sieves**) an object with lots of tiny holes, through which you strain food: Pass the soup through a fine sieve.

sigh verb (**sighs; sighing; sighed**) let out a long, slow breath because you are annoyed, bored, or unhappy.

sight noun the ability to see.

signature noun (plural **signatures**) the special way that you write your own name.

silent adjective making no sound.

silk noun a kind of soft, smooth cloth made from threads spun by silkworms.

silly adjective (**sillier; silliest**) foolish; not sensible: a silly mistake.

silver noun a valuable, shiny, grayish-white metal.

similar adjective being like someone or something in some way: A donkey is similar to a horse but smaller.

simple adjective (**simpler; simplest**) **1** easy to understand or do: a simple explanation. **2** plain; not fancy: a simple black dress.

sing verb (**sings; singing; sang; sung**) make music with your voice.

single adjective **1** only one of something: There was a single banana in the fruit bowl. **2** not married.

sink noun (plural **sinks**) a large basin with water taps and a drain.

+ verb (**sinks; sinking; sank; sunk**) go down below the surface of water.

sip verb (**sips; sipping; sipped**) take a small drink of something.

siren noun (plural **sirens**) something that makes a long, loud noise as a warning: We heard the siren of the fire engine.

sister noun (plural **sisters**) a woman or girl who has the same parents as you.

skate noun (plural **skates**) an ice skate or roller skate.

skateboard noun (plural **skateboards**) a board with small wheels underneath, which you stand on to ride.

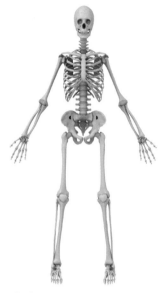

skeleton noun (plural **skeletons**) the bones in your body all joined together.

sketch noun (plural **sketches**) a rough drawing.

ski noun (plural **skis**) one of a pair of long, narrow pieces of light wood, metal, or plastic that you attach to boots, used for sliding over snow.

skill noun (plural **skills**) the ability to do something well.

skin noun (plural **skins**) 1 the thin layer that covers your body: A baby's skin is very soft. 2 the tough outer covering of a fruit or vegetable.

skip verb (**skips; skipping; skipped**) 1 move along while taking little jumps. 2 swing a rope over your head and around in a circle, jumping over it.

skirt noun (plural **skirts**) a piece of clothing that hangs down from the waist, which girls and women wear.

sky noun the space above the earth, where we see the sun, the moon, and the stars.

slack adjective (**slacker; slackest**) loose; not tight.

slam verb (**slams; slamming; slammed**) close a door hard so that it makes a loud bang.

slang noun words that you use when you are talking to your friends but not when you are writing or being polite.

slant verb (**slants; slanting; slanted**) be at an angle; slope.

sled noun (plural **sleds**) a kind of vehicle on long pieces of metal or wood used for sliding over snow or ice.

sleep verb (**sleeps; sleeping; slept**) rest your body and mind with your eyes closed.

sleeve noun (plural **sleeves**) the part of a piece of clothing that covers your arm or the top part of your arm.

sleigh noun (plural **sleighs**) a large sled that is pulled by animals.

slice noun (plural **slices**) a thin piece of food that has been cut off: a slice of bread. + verb (**slices; slicing; sliced**) cut food into thin slices.

slide verb (**slides; sliding; slid**) move smoothly over a surface: The car slid on the ice. + noun (plural **slides**) a piece of equipment that children play on in a playground, climbing up stairs to the top and then sliding down.

slight adjective (**slighter; slightest**) small; not severe: a slight headache.

slim adjective (**slimmer; slimmest**) slender or thin.

slip verb (**slips; slipping; slipped**) 1 slide and lose your balance. 2 go somewhere quickly and quietly: We slipped out without anyone noticing.

slipper noun (plural **slippers**) one of a pair of light shoes that you wear indoors.

slope noun (plural **slopes**) a piece of ground that is at an angle; slant.

slow adjective (**slower; slowest**) 1 not moving or not able to move quickly. 2 (of a clock etc.) showing a time later than what is correct.

sly adjective (**slyer; slyest**) clever at tricking people to get what you want.

small adjective (**smaller; smallest**) little; not big: a small dog.

smart adjective (**smarter; smartest**) 1 able to learn and understand things quickly; clever. 2 neat and well-dressed.

smash verb (**smashes; smashing; smashed**) break into many pieces, making a loud noise.

smell verb (**smells; smelling; smelled** or **smelt**) **1** notice something with your nose. **2** have a particular kind of smell: The roses smell lovely. ✛ noun (plural **smells**) **1** the ability to smell. **2** something that you can notice with your nose: There's a nasty smell in here.

smile verb (**smiles; smiling; smiled**) make your lips go up at the corners because you are happy.

smoke noun gray or black gas that comes from something that is burning.

smooth adjective (**smoother; smoothest**) flat or even; not rough or lumpy: This cream will keep your skin soft and smooth.

snack noun (plural **snacks**) a small amount of food that you eat between meals.

snail noun (plural **snails**) a small, slow-moving animal with no legs and a hard shell on its back.

snake noun (plural **snakes**) a long, thin animal with scales on its body and no legs.

sneeze verb (**sneezes; sneezing; sneezed**) force air suddenly out of your nose, making a loud noise.

sniff verb (**sniffs; sniffing; sniffed**) breathe in loudly through your nose.

snore verb (**snores; snoring; snored**) breathe very noisily while you sleep.

snow noun small, soft flakes of frozen water that fall from the sky in very cold weather.

snowball noun (plural **snowballs**) a hard ball made of snow pressed together.

snowman noun (plural **snowmen**) a figure of a man made of snow pressed together.

soak verb (**soaks; soaking; soaked**) make someone or something very wet.

soap noun a substance that you use with water to wash yourself.

sob verb (**sobs; sobbing; sobbed**) cry noisily.

soccer noun a game that is played between two teams who try to score goals by kicking a ball into a net.

sock noun (plural **socks**) one of a pair of soft coverings that you wear on your feet.

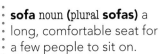

sofa noun (plural **sofas**) a long, comfortable seat for a few people to sit on.

soft adjective (**softer; softest**) **1** not hard or firm to the touch: a soft cushion. **2** (of a sound) not loud or harsh.

software noun computer programs.

soil noun the top layer of earth, where plants can grow.

soldier noun (plural **soldiers**) a member of an army.

solid noun (plural **solids**) any substance that is not a liquid or a gas: solids such as wood, metal, and stone. ✛ adjective **1** hard and firm to the touch: a solid oak door. **2** not hollow: a solid chocolate egg.

somersault noun (plural **somersaults**) rolling your whole body forward or backward on the floor.

son noun (plural **sons**) a male child.

song noun (plural **songs**) a piece of music with words for singing.

sore adjective (**sorer; sorest**) that causes pain: a sore foot.

sorry adjective (**sorrier**; **sorriest**) **1** feeling bad about something you have done: I'm sorry if I upset you. **2** feeling pity for someone: I felt sorry for the little girl who had lost all her money.

sound noun (plural **sounds**) something that you hear.

soup noun a hot liquid food made from vegetables and sometimes meat.

sour adjective (**sourer**; **sourest**) tasting sharp or bitter; not sweet: sour cherries.

south noun one of the four main points of the compass, to the right when you are facing the direction where the sun rises.

souvenir noun (plural **souvenirs**) something that you keep because it reminds you of a person or place that is important to you.

space noun (plural **spaces**) **1** an empty place: There is a space on the shelf where the book used to be. **2** the place above and around the earth, where the stars and planets are: traveling through space.

spaceship noun (plural **spaceships**) a vehicle that travels through space.

spade noun (plural **spades**) a tool with a long handle and a flat metal part used for digging.

spaghetti noun a kind of pasta in long, thin strands.

spare adjective that is in addition to what is needed; extra: Do you have a spare pen that I could borrow? + verb (**spares**; **sparing**; **spared**) have enough of something to be able to give some to someone else: Can you spare a couple of dollars?

sparkle verb (**sparkles**; **sparkling**; **sparkled**) shine brightly: Her diamond ring was sparkling.

sparrow noun (plural **sparrows**) a small brown bird.

speak verb (**speaks**; **speaking**; **spoke**; **spoken**) say something; talk.

spear noun (plural **spears**) a weapon consisting of a long pole with a sharp, pointed end.

special adjective **1** more important and better than other things or people: You are very special to me. **2** that is meant for a particular use: The firefighters used a special tool to cut open the car door.

spectator noun (plural **spectators**) a person who watches something, especially a sporting event.

speech noun (plural **speeches**) **1** the ability to speak. **2** a talk that someone gives to an audience.

speed noun (plural **speeds**) a measurement of how fast something is. + verb (**speeds**; **speeding**; **sped**) move very fast: He got into his car and sped off.

spell verb (**spells**; **spelling**; **spelled**) say or write the letters that make up a word in order. + noun (plural **spells**) in stories, a group of words that a character says that will affect someone in a magical way.

spend verb (**spends**; **spending**; **spent**) **1** use money to buy things. **2** pass time doing something.

sphere noun (plural **spheres**) a round, solid shape, like the shape of a ball.

spice noun (plural **spices**) a strong-tasting powder or seed used to add flavor to food.

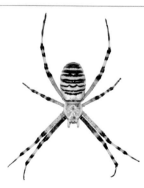

spider noun (plural **spiders**) a small creature with eight legs.

a b c d e f g h i j k l m n o p q r s t u v w x y z

spike noun (plural **spikes**) a long, thin piece of metal with a sharp point.

spill verb (**spills; spilling; spilled** or **spilt**) let a liquid fall out of a container accidentally.

spin verb (**spins; spinning; spun**) 1 turn around and around. 2 make thread from cotton or wool using a special machine. 3 (of a spider) make a web with a sticky thread that it produces from its body.

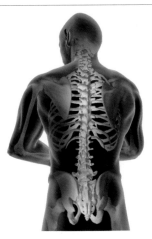

spine noun (plural **spines**) 1 the line of bones down the middle of your back. 2 one of the sharp, pointed parts on an animal's body or on a plant like a cactus.

spiteful adjective deliberately unpleasant to other people; nasty.

splash verb (**splashes; splashing; splashed**) disturb water so that it goes up in the air: The children were splashing about in the pool.

split verb (**splits; splitting; split**) 1 burst or crack: My shopping bag has split. 2 (of

two or more people) share something between them.

spoil verb (**spoils; spoiling; spoiled**) 1 ruin something: The sudden shower of rain spoiled the picnic. 2 give a child everything they want so that they become selfish and unpleasant.

sponge noun (plural **sponges**) 1 a piece of soft material with lots of small holes in it, which you use for washing yourself. 2 a soft; light cake.

sponsor verb (**sponsors; sponsoring; sponsored**) say that you will give someone money if they complete a task, such as a walk or swim, usually for charity.

spoon noun (plural **spoons**) a tool with a long handle and a shallow, rounded part that you use to eat soft food with, or to stir liquids with.

sport see page 100

spot noun (plural **spots**) 1 a small, round mark on something: a white shirt with blue spots. 2 a place: Let's find a quiet spot to have a picnic. verb (**spots; spotting; spotted**) see or notice something.
spotless adjective very clean.

spray verb (**sprays; spraying; sprayed**) wet something with small drops of water.

spread verb (**spreads; spreading; spread**) 1 open something out fully: Spread the map out on the table. 2 put a thin layer of butter or jam on a piece of bread, etc.

spring noun (plural **springs**) 1 the season between winter and summer, when plants start to grow. 2 a coil of wire that returns to its original shape after it has been pressed out of shape.
+ verb (**springs; springing; sprang; sprung**) jump up.

sprint verb (**sprints; sprinting; sprinted**) run fast for a short period.

spy noun (plural **spies**) a person who secretly finds out information about a person, country or organization.
verb (**spies; spying; spied**) 1 see or notice something. 2 secretly try to find out information about a person, country or organization.

square noun (plural **squares**) a shape with four sides of equal length and four right angles.

squash verb (**squashes; squashing; squashed**) press something so that it becomes flat.
+ noun (plural **squashes**) a plant related to the gourd that is usually eaten as a vegetable.

squeal verb (**squeals; squealing; squealed**) make a long, high-pitched sound.

squeeze verb (**squeezes; squeezing; squeezed**) press something hard from both sides.

squirrel noun (plural **squirrels**) a small, furry animal with a long, thick, bushy tail.

squirt verb (**squirts; squirting; squirted**) (of water) shoot out quickly in a thin stream.

stable noun (plural **stables**) a building where horses are kept.

stadium noun (plural **stadiums**) a large building where people go to watch sports.

sport
noun (plural **sports**) a game that you play that gives your body exercise: My favorite sport is hockey.

a b c d e f g h i j k l m n o p q r s t u v w x y z

running

soccer

football

high jump

basketball

cricket

gymnastics

bowling

tennis

squash

table tennis

volleyball

long jump

golf

beach volleyball

swimming

croquet

staff noun all the people who work for an organization.

stag noun (plural **stags**) a male deer.

stage noun (plural **stages**) a raised platform in a room or hall, where people sing, dance or act.

stain noun (plural **stains**) a dirty mark on something that is difficult to remove.

stair noun (plural **stairs**) a set of steps inside a building.

stale adjective (**staler; stalest**) (of food or air) not fresh.

stamp noun (plural **stamps**) a small piece of sticky paper with a picture on it, which you put on a letter or package that you are mailing to show that you have paid to mail it.
+ verb (**stamps; stamping; stamped**) put your foot down firmly on the ground.

stand verb (**stands; standing; stood**) **1** be upright on your feet. **2** tolerate or put up with someone or something: I can't stand bullies.

standard noun (plural **standards**) a measure of how good or bad something is: The singing in this competition is of a very high standard.
+ adjective ordinary or usual; not special: a standard size.

star noun (plural **stars**) **1** one of the small, bright lights that we see in the sky at night. **2** a shape that has five or more points sticking out. **3** a famous person, especially an entertainer or sportsperson.
+ verb (**stars; starring; starred**) (of an actor or actress) have the main part in a film, play, or television show.

stare verb (**stares; staring; stared**) look at someone or something for a long time.

start verb (**starts; starting; started**) begin to happen or begin to do something.

startle verb (**startles; startling; startled**) give someone a surprise or shock.

starve verb (**starves; starving; starved**) become ill or die because you do not have enough food.

station noun (plural **stations**) **1** a building where you go to catch a train or bus. **2** a building where firefighters or police officers work.

statue noun (plural **statues**) a sculpture of a person or animal.

steak noun (plural **steaks**) a thick slice of meat or fish.

steal verb (**steals; stealing; stole; stolen**) take something that belongs to someone else.

steam noun the hot gas that forms when water boils.

steel noun a strong metal made from iron.

steep adjective (**steeper; steepest**) (of a road, hill, or cliff) having a very sharp slope.

steer verb (**steers; steering; steered**) make a car or other vehicle go in a particular direction.

step noun (plural **steps**) **1** the movement you make when you lift and put down one foot when walking. **2** a raised flat surface that takes you from one level to another.

stew noun (plural **stews**) a mixture of meat and vegetables cooked for a long time in a saucepan.

stick noun (plural **sticks**) a thin piece of wood. **+** verb (**sticks; sticking; stuck**) **1** push a pin or other pointed object into something. **2** hold to something firmly: Rabia was stuck in the mud.

sticker noun (plural **stickers**) a small piece of paper with writing or a picture on one side and glue on the other side, which you can stick onto something.

sticky adjective (**stickier; stickiest**) that can stick to something: a sticky label.

stiff adjective (**stiffer; stiffest**) firm; not easily bent: a piece of stiff card.

stilt noun (plural **stilts**) one of a pair of long wooden or metal poles that you can walk on.

sting verb (**stings; stinging; stung**) (of an insect, plant, etc.) prick someone's skin, causing a sharp pain.

102

stir verb (**stirs; stirring; stirred**) move a spoon around in a container to mix together the food or drink that is in it.

stocking noun (plural **stockings**) one of a pair of long, thin coverings that a woman wears on her feet and legs.

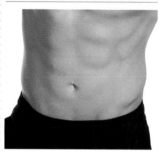

stomach noun (plural **stomachs**) the part inside your body that holds the food that you have eaten.

stone noun (plural **stones**) **1** the very hard material that rocks are made of. **2** a small piece of stone.

stool noun (plural **stools**) a seat with no back.

stop verb (**stops; stopping; stopped**) **1** no longer move: The car stopped at the lights. **2** no longer do something: Stop shouting!

storm noun (plural **storms**) a period of strong wind and heavy snow or rain, sometimes with thunder and lightning.

story noun (plural **stories**) **1** a description of something that has happened, whether made up or real: the story of Sleeping Beauty. **2** one of the floors of a tall building: the top story.

straight adjective (**straighter; straightest**) not bending or curving: a straight line.

strange adjective (**stranger; strangest**) **1** odd or unusual: I heard a strange noise. **2** not known to you: a strange city.

stranger noun (plural **strangers**) a person that

you do not know.

strap noun (plural **straps**) a band of leather or cloth used to fasten something or to hold things together.

straw noun (plural **straws**) **1** dried stems of wheat or other grain plants. **2** a small tube made of paper or plastic, which you put in a glass and suck a drink through.

strawberry noun (plural **strawberries**) a small, soft, red, juicy fruit.

stray adjective (of a dog or cat) that does not have an owner or live in a house.

stream noun (plural **streams**) **1** a small river. **2** a steady flow of people or things: a constant stream of visitors.

street noun (plural **streets**) a road in a town, with buildings on each side.

strength noun a measure of how strong someone or something is.

stretch verb (**stretches; stretching; stretched**) **1** make something longer or bigger: My sweater has gotten stretched in the wash. **2** reach your arms or legs out as far as you can.

strict adjective (**stricter; strictest**) insisting that other people follow the rules: a strict teacher.

stride verb (**strides; striding; strode; stridden**) walk with long steps. + noun (plural **strides**) a long step.

strike verb (**strikes; striking; struck**) hit someone or something. + noun (plural **strikes**) refusal by workers to work for a period of time, as a protest against poor pay or conditions.

string noun (plural **strings**) **1** a thin rope. **2** (on a guitar, violin, etc.) one of the long pieces of nylon or wire that produce sounds when you touch them.

strip noun (plural **strips**) a long, narrow piece of paper, cloth, etc. + verb (**strips; stripping; stripped**) take your clothes off.

stripe noun (plural **stripes**) a line of a color on a background of a different color.

stroke verb (**strokes; stroking; stroked**) rub

someone or something gently.

stroll verb (**strolls; strolling; strolled**) walk slowly.

strong adjective (**stronger; strongest**) **1** able to lift and carry heavy things; powerful. **2** that will not be easily broken or damaged; tough: a strong box. **3** (of a taste or smell) not mild: a strong smell of garlic.

struggle verb (**struggles; struggling; struggled**) **1** fight with all your strength: The baby was struggling to get out of his high chair. **2** try hard to do something difficult.

stubborn adjective very determined to do things your way.

student noun (plural **students**) a person who is studying at a school, college, or university.

study verb (**studies; studying; studied**) **1** learn about a subject, usually at school, college, or university. **2** look very closely at someone or something.

stumble verb (**stumbles; stumbling; stumbled**) trip and almost fall over.

stupid adjective (**stupider; stupidest**) not very smart.

subject noun (plural **subjects**) something that you learn about at school, college, or university: My favorite subject is art.

submarine noun (plural **submarines**) a ship that can travel underneath the water.

subtract verb (**subtracts; subtracting; subtracted**) in mathematics, take one number away from another: If you subtract 2 from 5, you get 3.

succeed verb (**succeeds; succeeding; succeeded**) manage to do what you were trying to do.

success noun managing to do what you were trying to do.

suck verb (**sucks; sucking; sucked**) pull liquid up into your mouth using your tongue and cheek muscles: She was sucking a milkshake through a straw.

sudden adjective happening quickly and with no warning: a sudden shower of rain.

suffer verb (**suffers; suffering; suffered**) be in pain or unhappy.

sugar noun a sweet substance added to food and drink to make it taste sweet.

suggest verb (**suggests; suggesting; suggested**) put a new idea or plan to someone: Mom suggested we go to the movies.

suit noun (plural **suits**) a set of matching clothes, either a jacket and pants or a jacket and skirt. + verb (**suits; suiting; suited**) look good on someone: That color suits you.

suitable adjective right for a particular purpose: suitable clothes for cold weather.

suitcase noun (plural **suitcases**) a container with a handle for carrying clothes and belongings in while traveling.

sum noun (plural **sums**) **1** an amount of money. **2** an exercise in arithmetic.

summer noun (plural **summers**) the season between spring and autumn; the warmest part of the year.

sunflower noun (plural **sunflowers**) a tall plant with large, yellow flowers.

sunglasses noun dark glasses that you wear to protect your eyes from the sun.

sunny adjective (**sunnier; sunniest**) bright and warm.

sunrise noun (plural **sunrises**) the time of day when the sun rises in the sky and it begins to get light.

sunset noun (plural **sunsets**) the time of day when the sun goes down and it begins to get dark.

sunshine noun the bright light from the sun.

someone and want them to do well.

suppose verb (**supposes; supposing; supposed**) think that something is true: I suppose they must be stuck in a traffic jam.

sure adjective (**surer; surest**) **1** having no doubt about something: I am sure Mom will be happy to see you. **2** certain to happen or to be as described; definite: The championship game is sure to be exciting.

surface noun (plural **surfaces**) the top or outer part of something: a wall with a rough surface.

sun noun the large, round object that shines in the sky during the day, which gives us heat and light.

sunburn noun red, sore skin resulting from being out in the sun for too long.

supermarket noun (plural **supermarkets**) a large shop that sells a lot of different foods and cleaning products, etc.

supper noun (plural **suppers**) a meal that you eat in the evening.

support verb (**supports; supporting; supported**) **1** hold someone or something up. **2** help

surgery noun (plural **surgeries**) medical treatment that involves cutting into the body: she had surgery to remove her appendix.

surname noun (plural **surnames**) your last name; your family name.

surprise noun (plural **surprises**) something unexpected that happens.

✦ verb (**surprises; surprising; surprised**) happen to someone unexpectedly.

surround verb (**surrounds; surrounding; surrounded**) be all around something or someone.

survive verb (**survives; surviving; survived**) live through a dangerous experience: He survived a plane crash.

suspect verb (**suspects; suspecting; suspected**) think that someone has done something wrong.

suspicious adjective **1** feeling unsure whether you can trust someone. **2** that makes people think you may have done something wrong.

swallow verb (**swallows; swallowing; swallowed**) make food or drink go from your mouth down your throat and into your stomach.
✦ noun (plural **swallows**) a small bird with a forked tail.

swap verb (**swaps; swapping; swapped**) give something to someone and get something from them in return: At the end of the game the players swapped shirts with the other team.

sweat verb (**sweats; sweating; sweated**) have a salty liquid come out of your skin because you are very hot.

sweater noun (plural **sweaters**) a knitted top with sleeves.

sweatshirt noun (plural **sweatshirts**) a warm top with sleeves, made of thick cotton.

sweep verb (**sweeps; sweeping; swept**) clean a floor with a brush.

sweet adjective (**sweeter; sweetest**) **1** (of food or drink) tasting of sugar. **2** (of a person) very nice.
✦ noun (plural **sweets**) food that tastes sweet: don't fill up on sweets.

swell verb (**swells; swelling; swelled; swollen**) become larger and more rounded.

swim verb (**swims; swimming; swam; swum**) move through water using your arms and legs.

swing verb (**swings; swinging; swung**) move backward and forward in the air.
✦ noun (plural **swings**) a seat hanging from a frame or from a tree, which you can move backward and forward when you sit in it.

switch noun (plural **switches**) a button or key that you press to turn on or off a piece of electrical equipment.
✦ verb (**switches; switching; switched**) press a switch to turn on or off a piece of electrical equipment: Switch the light off before you leave the room.

sword noun (plural **swords**) a weapon with a handle and a long, sharp blade.

sympathy noun a feeling of sharing someone else's sadness or suffering.

synagogue noun (plural **synagogues**) a place where Jews go to worship God.

T t

table noun (plural **tables**) **1** a piece of furniture consisting of a flat top held up by legs. **2** a list of facts or figures in rows or columns.

tail noun (plural **tails**) **1** the part that sticks out from the back of some kinds of animal, such as cats or dogs. **2** the back part of something: the tail of the plane.

tall adjective (**taller; tallest**) **1** (of a person) measuring a lot from head to feet. **2** (of a building, tree, etc.) high.

tame adjective (**tamer; tamest**) (of an animal) not wild; used to being with people and not afraid of them.

tan noun a darkening of the skin because you have been in the sun.

tea noun **1** a hot drink made from the leaves of the tea plant. **2** a party at which tea is served.

teach verb (**teaches; teaching; taught**) tell someone about something or show them how to do something.

team noun (plural **teams**) a group of people who work or play together.

tackle verb (**tackles; tackling; tackled**) **1** set about dealing with a difficult task. **2** in team sports, try to get the ball away from a player from the other team.

talcum powder noun a kind of fine, scented powder that you can put on your body.

tadpole noun (plural **tadpoles**) a tiny dark-colored creature with a round head and a long tail, which grows into a frog or toad.

tale noun (plural **tales**) a story.

talent noun (plural **talents**) a special ability to do something well.

tangle verb (**tangles; tangling; tangled**) twist hair, thread, etc., into a mess of knots.

target noun (plural **targets**) something that people aim at when shooting or throwing.

task noun (plural **tasks**) a piece of work that you have to do.

taste noun (plural **tastes**) **1** the flavor of something: a salty taste. **2** the ability to recognize flavors. ✦ verb (**tastes; tasting; tasted**) **1** (of food or a drink) have a particular kind of flavor: This salsa tastes very spicy. **2** eat or drink a little bit of something to see whether you like it.

taxi noun (plural **taxis**) a car that you can hire to take you somewhere.

tear verb (**tears; tearing; tore; torn**) pull something hard so that it splits; rip something. ✦ noun (plural **tears**) a drop of salty water that falls from your eyes when you cry.

tease verb (**teases; teasing; teased**) make fun of someone.

teddy bear noun (plural **teddy bears**) a soft, furry toy in the shape of a bear.

teenager (plural **teenagers**) a young person aged thirteen to nineteen.

telephone noun (plural **telephones**) an instrument that you use to talk to someone who is in another place.

telescope noun (plural **telescopes**) a piece of equipment that makes things that are far away look closer.

television noun (plural **televisions**) a piece of electrical equipment that you can watch programs on.

temper noun **1** an angry mood: He was in quite a temper. **2** a calm state of mind: She lost her temper.

temperature noun a measure of heat.

temple noun (plural **temples**) a building where some people go to worship God.

temporary adjective lasting for a short time: a temporary job.

tempt verb (**tempts; tempting; tempted**) encourage someone to do something that they should not do.

tennis noun a game in which players hit a ball backward and forward across a net, using a

special kind of bat called a racket.

tent noun (plural **tents**) a kind of shelter made of canvas or nylon stretched over poles, which you can sleep in.

term noun (plural **terms**) one of the parts that a school year is divided into.

terrify verb (**terrifies; terrifying; terrified**) frighten someone very badly.

test noun (plural **tests**) a set of questions to see how well you have learned something.
+ verb (**tests; testing; tested**) try something out to see how good it is.

text noun (plural **texts**) **1** a piece of writing. **2** a text message.
+ verb (**texts; texting; texted**) send a text message to someone.

text message noun (plural **text messages**) a message that you can write and send to

someone using your mobile phone.

thank verb (**thanks; thanking; thanked**) tell someone that you are grateful for something they have done for you or given you.

thaw verb (**thaws; thawing; thawed**) (of snow or ice) melt as the weather becomes warmer.

theater noun (plural **theaters**) a place where people go to see plays or shows.

thermometer noun (plural **thermometers**) something that measures the temperature of a person or a room.

thick adjective (**thicker; thickest**) **1** measuring a lot from one edge to the other: thick slices of bread. **2** (of a liquid) not runny or watery: thick cream.

thief noun (plural **thieves**) someone who steals things from other people.

thigh noun (plural **thighs**) the top part of your leg, above the knee.

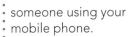

thin adjective **(thinner; thinnest) 1** not measuring much from edge to edge: *peppers cut in thin strips.* **2** (of a person) not weighing a lot; not fat. **3** (of a liquid) runny or watery.

thirsty adjective **(thirstier; thirstiest)** feeling the need for a drink.

thistle noun (plural **thistles)** a wild plant with purple flowers and prickly leaves.

thorn noun (plural **thorns)** a sharp point on the stem of a plant such as a rose.

thread noun (plural **threads)** a long, thin piece of cotton or silk that you use for sewing. **+** verb **(threads; threading; threaded)** put a piece of thread through the hole in a needle.

throat noun (plural **throats)** the part at the back of your mouth where food and drink goes when you swallow it.

throne noun (plural **thrones)** a special chair for a king or queen.

throw verb **(throws; throwing; threw; thrown)** make something fly through the air from your hand: *The boys were throwing snowballs at each other.*

thud noun (plural **thuds)** a dull, heavy sound: *The books fell on the floor with a thud.*

thumb noun (plural **thumbs)** the short, thick finger at one side of your hand.

thunder noun the loud, banging sound that you hear before a flash of lightning during a thunderstorm.

ticket noun (plural **tickets)** a small piece of printed paper or card that shows you have paid to travel on a bus, train, etc., or to attend the theater, movies, or a sporting event.

tickle verb **(tickles; tickling; tickled)** touch someone lightly with your fingertips to make them laugh.

tide noun (plural **tides)** the changing of the level of the sea that happens twice a day.

tidy adjective **(tidier; tidiest)** neat; not messy. **+** verb **(tidies; tidying; tidied)** make a room tidy.

tiger noun (plural **tigers)** a large wild animal of the cat family with striped fur.

tight adjective **(tighter; tightest)** (of a piece of clothing) fitting closely; not loose: *My shoes hurt my feet because they are too tight.*

tights noun a thin piece of clothing that a woman or girl wears on her feet, legs, and bottom.

timetable noun (plural **timetables)** a list of times when trains or buses leave or of when things are planned to happen.

timid adjective shy and easily frightened.

tin noun (plural **tins) 1** a soft, silvery metal. **2** a metal container holding food or a drink: *a tin of cookies.*

tiny adjective **(tinier; tiniest)** very small.

tiptoe verb **(tiptoes; tiptoeing; tiptoed)** walk quietly on the tips of your toes.

tire noun (plural **tires)** a ring of thick, strong rubber that fits round the outside edge of a wheel.

tired adjective **1** feeling the need for sleep. **2** bored or annoyed with something: *I'm tired of this cold weather.*

title noun (plural **titles) 1** the name of a book, film, etc. **2** a word that goes before someone's name, such Mrs., Mr., Sir, or Dr.

toad noun (plural **toads)** an animal that looks like a big frog but with drier skin, which lives mainly on land.

a b c d e f g h i j k l m n o p q r s t u v w x y z

toadstool noun (plural **toadstools**) a small plant with a thick stem and a round top, which looks like a mushroom but which is poisonous to eat.

toast noun bread that has been heated until it becomes brown and crisp.

toddler noun (plural **toddlers**) a very young child that has just learned to walk.

toe noun (plural **toes**) one of the parts that stick out from the ends of your feet.

tomato noun (plural **tomatoes**) a small, soft, round, red fruit that can be eaten raw or cooked.

tongue noun (plural **tongues**) the part inside your mouth that you can move around and that you use for eating and speaking.

tool noun (plural **tools**) something, such as a saw or a hammer, that you use to do a job.

tooth noun (plural **teeth**) **1** one of the hard white parts of your mouth, which you use for biting and chewing. **2** one of the pointed parts of a comb or saw.

toothbrush noun (plural **toothbrushes**) a small brush for cleaning your teeth.

top noun (plural **tops**) **1** the highest part of something: the top of the mountain. **2** the lid of a bottle, jar, etc. **3** a piece of clothing, such as a T-shirt or sweater, that you wear on the top part of your body.

topic noun (plural **topics**) a subject that you talk or write about.

torch noun (plural **torches**) flaming light that burns brightly and is carried in the hand.

tortoise noun (plural **tortoises**) a small, slow-moving animal with four legs and a hard shell on its back.

total noun (plural **totals**) the result you get when you add numbers together.
+ adjective complete or absolute: a total disaster.

touch verb (**touches**; **touching**; **touched**) **1** feel something with your hand. **2** (of two things) be next to each other or joined onto each other.

tough adjective (**tougher**; **toughest**) **1** (of meat) hard to cut or to chew. **2** hard to break or to damage. **3** (of a person) strong and capable.

tour noun (plural **tours**) a trip to various different places: a tour of Europe.

tourist noun (plural **tourists**) a person who visits a place on vacation.

tournament noun (plural **tournaments**) a set of games in which the winning person or team plays in the next game until only one person or team is left.

towel noun (plural **towels**) a piece of soft cloth that you dry yourself with.

tower noun (plural **towers**) a tall, narrow building.

town noun (plural **towns**) a place where a lot of people live, which is smaller than a city but bigger than a village.

toy noun (plural **toys**) something that children play with.

tractor noun (plural **tractors**) a strong farm vehicle with large wheels that is used for pulling and lifting heavy things.

trampoline noun (plural **trampolines**) a piece of strong material that is attached to a frame with springs, which you can bounce up and down on.

traffic noun all the vehicles that travel on the roads: There is heavy traffic on the highway.

transparent adjective that you can see through: a transparent plastic cover.

transportation see page 111

treasure noun (plural **treasures**) a collection of valuable things such as jewels or gold and silver objects.

treat verb (**treats; treating; treated**) **1** behave in a particular way toward a person or animal: The dog had been badly treated by its last owner. **2** (of a doctor or nurse) take care of a sick person and help them become well again.

treat noun (plural **treats**) something special that someone enjoys.

tree noun (plural **trees**) a very tall plant with a strong trunk, branches, and leaves.

tremble verb (**trembles; trembling; trembled**) shake because you are cold or afraid.

train noun (plural **trains**) a vehicle consisting of an engine pulling carriages, which travels on a railway. + verb (**trains; training; trained**) **1** teach a person or animal a skill. **2** do exercises to prepare for a sport: She is training for the marathon.

trainer noun (plural **trainers**) **1** a person who trains people or animals.

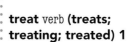

trap noun (plural **traps**) something that is used to catch a person or animal.

travel verb (**travels; traveling; traveled**) go from one place to another.

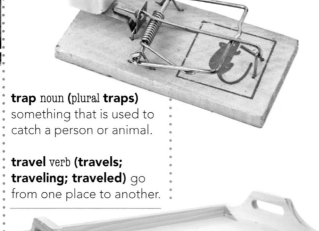

tray noun (plural **trays**) a flat board with raised edges, which is used for carrying food and drinks.

triangle noun (plural **triangles**) a shape with three straight sides and three angles.

transportation

noun a system or means of carrying people or things from one place to another.

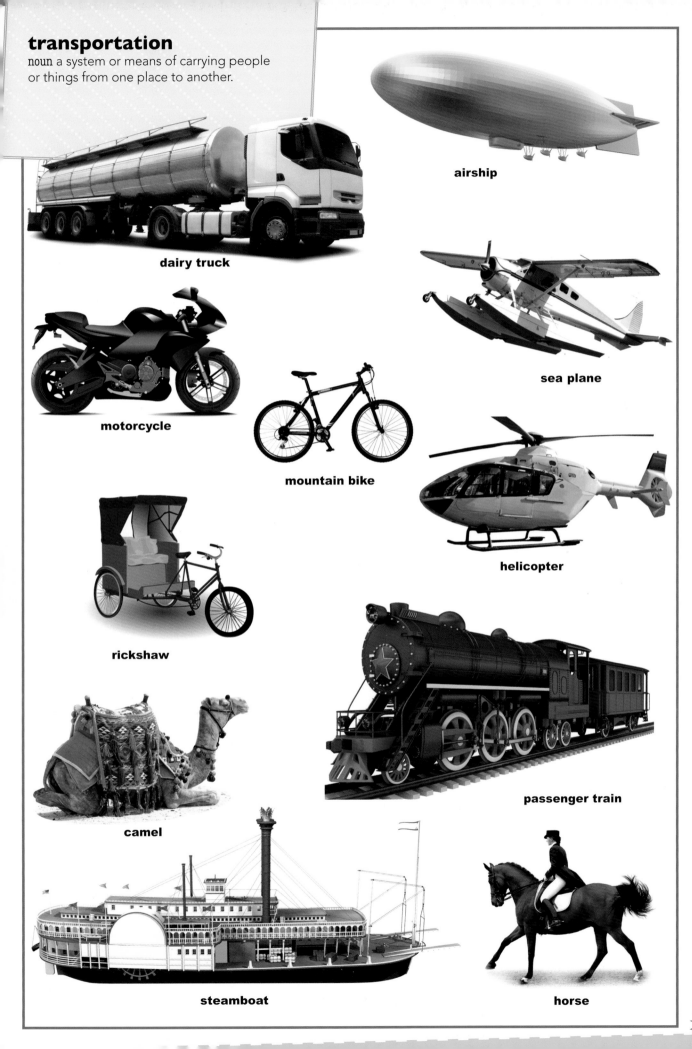

dairy truck

airship

motorcycle

sea plane

mountain bike

helicopter

rickshaw

camel

passenger train

steamboat

horse

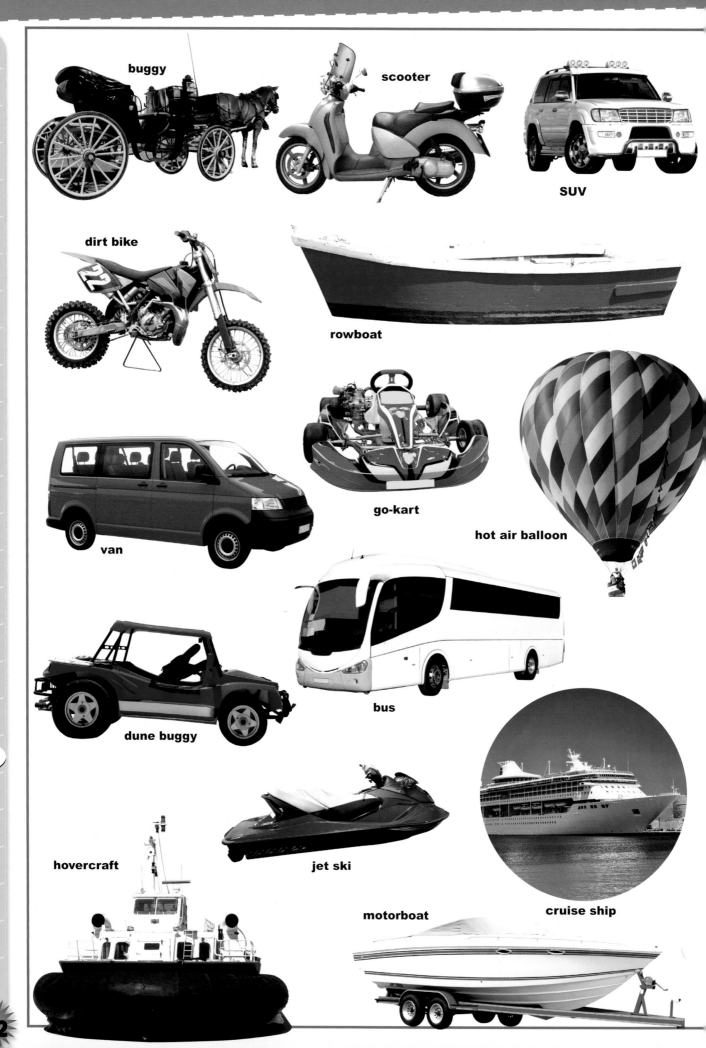

buggy

scooter

SUV

dirt bike

rowboat

van

go-kart

hot air balloon

dune buggy

bus

hovercraft

jet ski

motorboat

cruise ship

vintage car

race car

jeep

yacht

limousine

hang glider

motor home

double decker bus

all-terrain
vehicle

sailboat

tricycle noun (plural **tricycles**) a vehicle with three wheels and no engine, which you pedal with your feet.

trip noun (plural **trips**) a journey: We went on a trip to California.

trolley noun (plural **trolleys**) streetcar that runs on tracks and gets its power through electricity.

trophy noun (plural **trophies**) something, such as a cup, that you win as a prize in a competition.

trousers noun pants; a piece of clothing that covers your legs and bottom.

trout noun (plural **trout**) a fish that lives in lakes and rivers and that people can eat.

true adjective (**truer; truest**) real; not false.

trumpet noun (plural **trumpets**) a brass musical instrument that you play by blowing into it.

trunk noun (plural **trunks**) **1** the strong, hard, main part of a tree, which the branches grow out from. **2** the very long nose of an elephant. **3** a large, strong box with a lid, used for storing things.

trust verb (**trusts; trusting; trusted**) believe that someone is honest and reliable.

truth noun something that is true: If you tell the truth about what happened, you won't get into trouble.

T-shirt noun (plural **T-shirts**) a cotton top with short sleeves.

tube noun (plural **tubes**) **1** a long, rounded, hollow object. **2** a long, thin container with a lid that you can squeeze the contents out of: a tube of toothpaste.

tulip noun (plural **tulips**) a colorful, cup-shaped flower that blooms in the spring.

tuna noun a large fish that lives in warm areas and that people can eat.

tune noun (plural **tunes**) a group of musical notes that together make a nice sound.

tunnel noun (plural **tunnels**) a long passage under the ground that people can walk or drive through.

turkey noun (plural **turkeys**) a large bird that is kept on a farm for its meat.

turtle noun (plural **turtles**) an animal with a hard shell on its back, which lives on land, in water, or both.

tusk noun (plural **tusks**) one of a pair of very long, pointed teeth that elephants and walruses have.

TV noun (plural **TVs**) a television.

twig noun (plural **twigs**) a very small, thin branch of a tree.

twin noun (plural **twins**) one of two children that are born to the same mother at the same time.

twist verb (**twists; twisting; twisted**) **1** change the shape of something by bending or turning it around. **2** turn something around: Twist the lid off the jar.

typical adjective usual or ordinary; as you would expect: He's a typical teenager.

Uu

ugly adjective (**uglier; ugliest**) not pleasant to look at.

umbrella noun (plural **umbrellas**) a covered frame on a stick that you hold over your head to protect you from the rain.

uncle noun (plural **uncles**) your mother's or father's brother, or your aunt's husband.

uncomfortable adjective not easy to wear or to use: uncomfortable shoes.

underground adjective that is below the surface of the ground: an underground tunnel.
+ noun (plural **undergrounds**) a railway that runs in tunnels below the surface of the ground.

underline verb (**underlines; underlining; underlined**) draw a line under a word or phrase.

understand verb (**understands; understanding; understood**) know what something means.

undo verb (**undoes; undoing; undid; undone**) unfasten something: Her shoelaces were undone.

undress verb (**undresses; undressing; undressed**) take off your clothes.

unfortunate adjective having bad luck or happening as a result of bad luck; unlucky.

unhappy adjective (**unhappier; unhappiest**) feeling sad.

unhealthy adjective (**unhealthier; unhealthiest**) **1** (of a person) unfit or unwell. **2** bad for your health: an unhealthy lifestyle.

uniform noun (plural **uniforms**) a special set of clothes that is worn by all the people in a particular organization: children in school uniform.

unique adjective being the only one of a kind.

unit noun (plural **units**) **1** something that is used for measuring something: a unit of electricity. **2** in mathematics, the number one: hundreds, tens, and units.

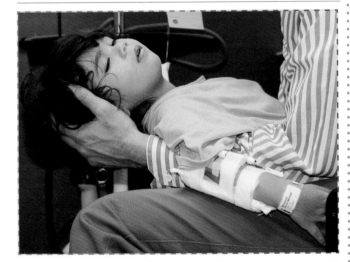

unconscious adjective not awake or aware of what is going on around you: The patient is still unconscious after bumping his head.

unemployed adjective having no job.

unfair adjective not treating everyone equally: unfair treatment.

unicorn noun (plural **unicorns**) in stories, an animal that looks like a white horse with a horn on its head.

universe noun all of space, including the sun and all the stars and planets.

university noun (plural **universities**) a place where some people go to study after they have graduated from high school.

unlikely adjective (**unlikelier; unlikeliest**) not probable: It looks unlikely that our team will win.

unpack verb (**unpacks; unpacking; unpacked**) take out the things that are packed in a suitcase or bag.

unpleasant adjective not nice, pleasing, or enjoyable: an unpleasant surprise.

untidy adjective (**untidier; untidiest**) not clean and neat; messy.

unusual adjective strange or rare; not ordinary.

upright adjective standing up straight.

upset verb (**upsets; upsetting; upset**) **1** make someone feel sad or worried. **2** knock something over. + adjective sad or crying.

upside-down adjective having been turned so that the top is at the bottom.

urgent adjective that needs to be dealt with immediately: an urgent repair.

useful adjective helpful: useful information.

useless adjective **1** that cannot be used: a useless gadget. **2** not helpful: He is completely useless around the house.

usual adjective happening, done, or used most often: my usual routine.

Vv

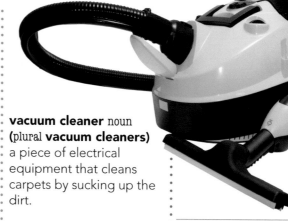

vacuum cleaner noun (plural **vacuum cleaners**) a piece of electrical equipment that cleans carpets by sucking up the dirt.

vain adjective (**vainer; vainest**) **1** very proud of your appearance. **2** unsuccessful: a vain attempt.

valuable adjective **1** worth a lot of money. **2** (of advice or help) very useful.

vaccination noun (plural **vaccinations**) putting medicine into someone's body using a special needle.

valley noun (plural **valleys**) an area of low land between two hills.

vegetable

noun (plural **vegetables**) plants or parts of plants that can be eaten.

potato

cauliflower

asparagus

radish

celery

cucumber

onions

bell pepper

spinach

lettuce

turnip

beet

peas

carrot

broccoli

cabbage

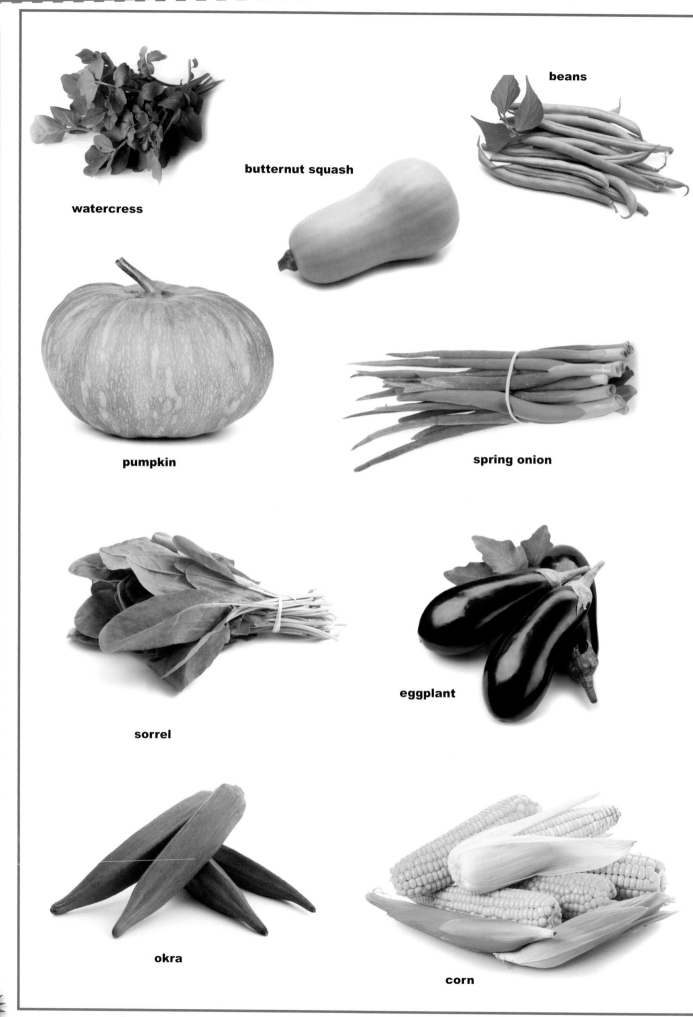

watercress

butternut squash

beans

pumpkin

spring onion

sorrel

eggplant

okra

corn

artichoke

sweet potato

parsnips

brussels sprouts

radicchio

mushroom

chicory

watercress

leek

chard

vandal noun (plural **vandals**) a person who deliberately damages other people's property or public property.

vanilla noun a kind of flavoring for ice cream, cakes, etc.

vanish verb (**vanishes; vanishing; vanished**) disappear.

vegetable see page 117

vegetarian noun (plural **vegetarians**) a person who eats no meat or fish.

vehicle noun (plural **vehicles**) a machine that is a method of transport, such as a car, bus, or train.

veil noun (plural **veils**) a piece of thin material that is worn over the head or face by some women.

vein noun (plural **veins**) one of the narrow tubes inside your body that carry blood to your heart.

velvet noun a kind of thick, very soft cloth.

verse noun (plural **verses**) **1** one of the divisions of a song or poem: She sang the

first verse and the chorus. **2** poetry: a book of verse.

vertical adjective standing straight up or pointing straight up: vertical stripes.

vessel noun (plural **vessels**) a ship or boat.

vet noun (plural **vets**) a doctor who treats animals.

via preposition by way of; through: We went to home via a shortcut.

victim noun (plural **victims**) a person who has been harmed by someone or something: a victim of crime.

victory noun (plural **victories**) success in a battle, game, or a contest.

view noun (plural **views**) what you can see from a particular place: a beautiful view from the balcony.

vinegar noun a sour-tasting liquid that is added to food for flavor.

violent adjective **1** (of a person) using physical force against other people. **2** (of a storm, argument, etc.) forceful and possibly harmful.

village noun (plural **villages**) a small town.

violin noun (plural **violins**) a musical instrument with strings, which you hold under your chin and play with a bow.

visit verb (**visits; visiting; visited**) **1** go to see someone in their house or in hospital. **2** go to see a place: We visited the art museum.

vitamin noun (plural **vitamins**) something that is in food that you need to stay healthy.

voice noun (plural **voices**) the sound that you make when you speak or sing.

volcano noun (plural **volcanoes**) a mountain that sometimes throws hot liquid rock and ash out of a hole in the top.

volume noun (plural **volumes**) **1** a book, especially one of a set. **2** the amount of space that an object takes up; size. **3** a degree of loudness: Turn down the volume of the television.

volunteer verb (**volunteers; volunteering; volunteered**) offer to do something without being told to and without being paid.

✦ noun (plural **volunteers**) a person who offers to do something without being told to and without being paid.

vote verb (**votes; voting; voted**) say which person or thing you choose from a range of choices, often by raising your hand or making a mark on a piece of paper.

vulture noun (plural **vultures**) a large bird that eats dead animals.

W w

wafer noun (plural **wafers**) a thin, crisp cracker or cookie, sometimes eaten with ice cream.

waist noun (plural **waists**) the narrowest part in the middle of your body.

waiter noun (plural **waiters**) a man who takes orders and serves food in a restaurant.

waitress noun (plural **waitresses**) a woman who takes orders and serves food in a restaurant.

walk verb (**walks; walking; walked**) move along by putting one foot in front of the other.
✦ noun (plural **walks**) moving along by putting one foot in front of the other: a walk in the park.

wallet noun (plural **wallets**) a small folding case to keep your money in.

wallpaper noun (plural **wallpapers**) a kind of thick paper, often with a pattern, that you stick on the walls of a room.

walrus noun (plural **walruses**) a sea creature that looks like a large seal with two long tusks.

wand noun (plural **wands**) **1** in stories, a special stick that a fairy or wizard waves around when casting a spell. **2** a special stick that a magician waves around when doing magic tricks.

wander verb (**wanders; wandering; wandered**) walk around in no particular direction.

war noun (plural **wars**) a time of fighting between countries.

wardrobe noun (plural **wardrobes**) a cupboard where you hang your clothes.

warm adjective (**warmer; warmest**) slightly hot.

warn verb (**warns; warning; warned**) tell someone that they might be in danger.

wasp noun (plural **wasps**) a flying insect with yellow and black stripes on its body, which can sting you.

wash verb (**washes; washing; washed**) clean something or clean yourself with soap and water.

watch verb (**watches; watching; watched**) look at something for a while: The children are watching a movie.
+ noun (plural **watches**) a small clock that you wear on your wrist.

water noun a clear liquid that falls as rain and forms rivers, lakes, and seas, and which we use for drinking and washing.
+ verb (**waters; watering; watered**) pour water on a plant to keep it alive.

waterfall noun (plural **waterfalls**) a place where water from a river falls over a ledge onto the ground below.

wave verb (**waves; waving; waved**) **1** move your hand from side to side as a way of saying hello or goodbye. **2** (of an object) move from side to side or up and down: The clothes were waving around on the clothesline.
+ noun (plural **waves**) a moving ridge on the surface of water.

wax noun a substance made from fat or oil, which is used to make candles and polish.

weak adjective (**weaker; weakest**) **1** not having much strength: The old lady was quite weak after her illness. **2** (of a drink) not having a strong taste: This tea is too weak.

wealthy adjective (**wealthier; wealthiest**) having a lot of money; rich.

weapon noun (plural **weapons**) something, such as a gun or a knife, that can be used to hurt or kill people.

weary adjective (**wearier; weariest**) very tired.

weather noun the conditions outside, including how hot or cold it is and whether it is raining, snowing, or sunny.

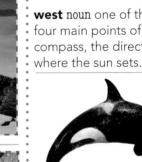

web noun (plural **webs**) **1** a fine net that a spider makes to catch insects. **2** the World Wide Web, a large collection of information that is stored on computers all over the world and linked by the Internet.

wedding noun (plural **weddings**) marriage ceremony and celebration.

weed noun (plural **weeds**) a kind of wild plant that grows where it is not wanted: There were weeds growing in the cracks in the garden path.

weekend noun (plural **weekends**) Saturday and Sunday.

weep verb (**weeps; weeping; wept**) have tears coming out of your eyes, often because you are sad; cry.

weight noun the measurement of how heavy a person or thing is.

weird adjective (**weirder; weirdest**) strange and slightly frightening.

welcome verb (**welcomes; welcoming; welcomed**) show someone that you are happy to see them when they arrive.

west noun one of the four main points of the compass, the direction where the sun sets.

whale noun (plural **whales**) a very large sea creature that looks like a huge fish, which breathes through a hole in the top of its head.

wheat noun a plant that is grown for its seeds, which are called grain and which are used to make flour.

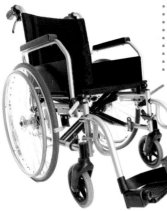

wheel noun (plural **wheels**) one of the round objects that turn around and which vehicles move on.

wheelchair noun (plural **wheelchairs**) a special chair on large wheels for people who cannot walk very well or at all.

whip noun (plural **whips**) a long, thin piece of leather or rope with a handle, which can be used to hit an animal or person.

+ verb (**whips; whipping; whipped**) **1** hit an animal or person with a whip. **2** beat cream or eggs until they are thick or stiff.

whisker noun (plural **whiskers**) one of the stiff hairs that stick out from the sides of a cat's or other animal's mouth.

whisper verb (**whispers; whispering; whispered**) speak very quietly.

whistle noun (plural **whistles**) a small object that you blow into to make a loud, high-pitched sound.
+ verb (**whistles; whistling; whistled**) make a loud, high-pitched sound by blowing air through your lips or by blowing into a whistle.

white adjective (**whiter; whitest**) of the palest color, like snow.
+ noun (plural **whites**) the clear part of an egg, which turns white when it is cooked.

wicked adjective very bad or cruel.

wide adjective (**wider; widest**) measuring a lot from side to side.

wife noun (plural **wives**) a female partner in a marriage.

wig noun (plural **wigs**) false hair that you wear on your head.

wild adjective (**wilder; wildest**) **1** (of an animal or plant) living and growing naturally, without being looked after by people. **2** (of behavior) uncontrolled and energetic.

willing adjective prepared and happy to do something: Lucy is always willing to share her toys with the other children.

win verb (**wins; winning; won**) beat the other people or teams in a game or competition.

wind noun (plural **winds**) a fast-moving current of air.
+ verb (**winds; winding; wound**) **1** twist something around itself or around something else. **2** (of a road or river) have lots of bends.

window noun (plural **windows**) a space in a wall or in a car, filled with glass, which lets light in and which you can see through.

windshield noun (plural **windshields**) the window in the front of a vehicle.

wing noun (plural **wings**) **1** one of the parts of a bird or insect that it flaps

124

to make it fly. **2** one of the two long parts of an airplane that stick out at either side.

wink verb **(winks; winking; winked)** close and open one eye quickly.

winter noun **(plural winters)** the season between autumn and spring, the coldest part of the year.

wise adjective **(wiser; wisest)** experienced and sensible.

wish verb **(wishes; wishing; wished)** want something to happen: I wish I had a puppy.

witch noun **(plural witches)** in fairy tales, a woman with magic powers.

witness noun **(plural witnesses)** a person who sees something happen, especially a crime or an accident.

wizard noun **(plural wizards)** in fairy tales, a man with magic powers.

wobble verb **(wobbles; wobbling; wobbled)** move slightly from side to side.

wolf noun **(plural wolves)** a wild animal with gray fur that looks like a large dog.

wonderful adjective amazing and marvelous.

wood noun **(plural woods) 1** the substance that trees are made of, which is used to make furniture, etc. **2** an area of land with lots of trees growing close together.

wool noun the soft, thick hair that grows on a sheep's body and is used to make sweaters and other clothes.

word noun **(plural words)** a group of letters or sounds that has a meaning.

work verb **(works; working; worked) 1** do something useful, especially as a job. **2** (of a machine, etc.) operate properly: My computer is not working.
+ noun the tasks that you have to do.

world noun the planet we live on; the earth.

worm noun **(plural worms)** a small creature with a long, thin body and no legs.

worry verb **(worries; worrying; worried)** be anxious and afraid that something bad might happen.

worship verb **(worships; worshipping; worshipped)** show love and respect to God or a god, for example by praying.

worth adjective **1** having a certain value in money: This painting is worth $1000. **2** having a certain importance, usefulness or quality: This book is really worth reading.

wound noun **(plural wounds)** an injury to the body, especially a cut.
+ verb **(wounds; wounding; wounded)** injure someone.

wrap verb **(wraps; wrapping; wrapped)** cover something tightly with paper or cloth.

wrapper noun (plural **wrappers**) a piece of paper or other material that something you buy is wrapped in.

wrestle verb (**wrestles; wrestling; wrestled**) fight with someone by trying to force them down onto the floor, but without hitting or kicking them.

wriggle verb (**wriggles; wriggling; wriggled**) twist your body from side to side.

wrinkle noun (plural **wrinkles**) a small line in your skin that appears as you get older.

write verb (**writes; writing; wrote; written**) put words onto a piece of paper using a pen or pencil.

wreck verb (**wrecks; wrecking; wrecked**) destroy something completely.
+ noun (plural **wrecks**) a vehicle that has been destroyed in an accident.

wrist noun (plural **wrists**) the narrow part where your arm joins your hand.

wrong adjective **1** not correct or accurate: the wrong answer. **2** bad; not right: Telling lies is wrong.

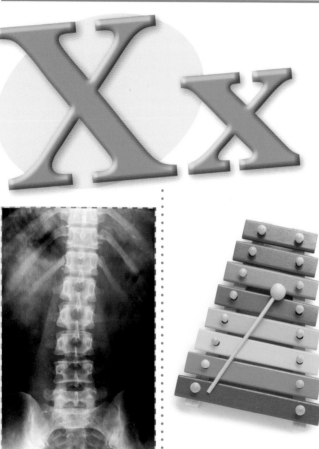

yacht noun (plural **yachts**) a sailing boat used for racing or for pleasure.

yawn verb (**yawns; yawning; yawned**) open your mouth wide and breathe in deeply because you are tired or bored.

year noun (plural **years**) a period of 365 days, divided into 52 weeks or 12 months.

xylophone noun (plural **xylophones**) a musical instrument with a row of metal or wooden bars that each make a different sound when you hit them with special hammers.

X-ray noun (plural **X-rays**) a special kind of photograph that shows the insides of your body so that doctors can see if there is anything wrong.

yellow adjective of the color of lemons.

yogurt noun (plural **yogurts**) a thick liquid food made from milk, with a slightly sour taste.

yolk noun (plural **yolks**) the yellow part in the middle of an egg.

young adjective (**younger; youngest**) having lived for a short time; not old.

youth noun (plural **youths**) **1** a young person. **2** the time of your life when you are young.

yo-yo noun (plural **yo-yos**) a small, round toy on a string, which you loop around your finger and make the toy go up and down the string.

Zz

zebra noun (plural **zebras**) a wild animal that looks like a horse with black-and-white striped fur.

zero noun (plural **zeros**) nothing; the number 0.

zigzag noun (plural **zigzags**) a line with many sharp turns.

zoo noun (plural **zoos**) a place where many wild animals are kept so that people can go see them.

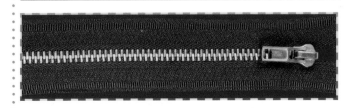

zipper noun (plural **zippers**) a kind of fastener on clothes and bags that has two rows of teeth that join together when you pull up a small clip.